This book is dedicated to anybody who's ever felt that there was no place for them.

Table of Contents

Part I: Personal Experiences

Chapter One

Chapter Two

Chapter Three

Chapter Four

Chapter Nine

Part III: Philosophical Aspects

Chapter Ten

Chapter Eleven

Chapter Twelve

Chapter Thirteen

Chapter Fourteen

Skirting Gender: Life and Lessons of a Cross Dresser

Hello there. My name is Vera Wylde. Well, not really. That's not the name on my birth certificate, my driver's license, or the bills that come to my home. Nor do I wish for that to be the name on any of those documents. But sometimes it's what I like to be called. Most of the time I'm a somewhat unremarkable, overtly geeky, cisgender male. I go to work, I buy groceries, and I take my child to the playground in what would generally be considered standard male attire (everybody's wearing Doctor Who hoodies these days, right?). But sometimes I like to wear a dress. And makeup. And maybe a wig. And I put on high heels, fill out a bra with fake breasts, and cinch my waist in with a corset. That's right, I'm a cross dresser. Nice to meet you.

I've written this book as a means of bringing insight to those who want to better understand cross dressing, be they dressers themselves, people with loved ones who dress, or just the idly curious. The book has been broken up into three sections: my personal experiences, practical advice, and the philosophical aspects of gender non-conformity. The first is fairly self-explanatory and covers the major points in my own life journey as a dresser. The second deals with the logistical things: hair, makeup, shopping, walking in heels, etc. And the final section touches on broader issues like who a dresser should come out to, distinguishing between gender and sexual preference, where dressers fit into the LGBTQ+ community, and other somewhat murky topics. It's in this last section that I also talk about some of the most recent turns in my life as they relate to everything else in the book. I hope you'll find this informative, or at least entertaining.

WHO IS VERA WYLDE?

You'd think that by this point in my life I could answer that question quickly and succinctly. It shouldn't be that hard. But the truth is I'm still not entirely sure of the answer myself. I know what Vera's public persona is. She's a burlesque drag queen and cross dressing advice video blogger. She's a model, a performer, and a bit of a tease. She's flirty, usually smiling, and tends to mug for the camera a bit. But that's just the surface level; that doesn't really tell anybody much of anything that they can't assess for themselves. It doesn't say who she is to me, or how she fits into my life.

So is she a character? A façade? Is she something that I use to hide behind? Or is she actually me? Is she a truer version of myself than the one I present in my day-to-day life as a man? Is she some manifestation of parts of my personality that I have to set aside most of the time? Did I create her or was she always there waiting to come out for the world to see? I have a few ideas on how to answer these questions, but in the end I have no firm answers. And for my part I've become comfortable with that.

For me Vera just is. She is me and yet she is somehow separate at the same time. She doesn't dominate my life, but I can't simply ignore her, nor would I want to. I think she's always been there in some way, though it took some time for her to truly take shape. Maybe I'll never know who Vera truly is. She seems to be constantly evolving, changing with each new experience. Just like the rest of us I suppose. Nobody stays the same; we are always changing. Vera is no different. And that's the paradox.

Because Vera is me, unquestionably and undeniably. She's not a "character," she's not the Madea to my daily life as Tyler Perry. I don't pretend to adopt traits I don't already have when I'm her, even though she brings out a different side of me. At the same time, it's true that she is her own person, with her own drives and needs. The things that thrill and energize the side of me that's embodied by Vera don't have the same effect on me in my day-to-day existence. Can somebody truly live a full life while trying to meet the needs of what might as well be two people within themselves? I like to think I've been handling it ok up to this point, but really who knows? Let's explore together.

Part I: Personal Experiences

CHAPTER ONE

EARLIEST DAYS

It's funny when I talk to other dressers about their earliest experiences. Some have such a clear memory of their first inclinations, the things that made them want to live at least a part of their lives as a woman. I call it the "Fay Wray Moment." Fans of the *Rocky Horror Picture Show* probably caught that reference right off the bat, but here's a little context for everybody else:

In this very wild cult musical, Tim Curry plays a transvestite and one of his last songs opens with him describing seeing actress Fay Wray (best known for starring in the original *King Kong*) and the way her clothes clung to her body. He sings that he knew at that moment he wanted to be dressed the same way. Maybe it's just my impression but it seems like a fair number of dressers have that Fay Wray Moment somewhere along the line, something they can point to as a bolt out of the blue that first planted the idea firmly in their heads and hearts that they wanted to look like women, or at least solidified their idealized version of what it meant to be feminine.

I never really had that. And I suppose the lack of such a moment is part of what makes it hard to say where any of this really started for me.

I have photographic proof that I dressed in girl's clothing as young as three years old, but honestly I don't give such an act all that much weight in the grand scheme of things. At the time those photos were taken, my mother and I were living in a duplex and the other half of the house was occupied by good friends of hers who had two daughters. They were both older than me, but we all played together. And naturally when we played dress up I ended up in a tutu from time to time, because that's what they had available. However, the fact that I have only hazy conscious memories of this causes me to not weigh it very heavily as a factor in my development as a dresser.

Proof that I've always been cute.

In a way, I suppose it was an influence because no one ever said to me or the girls that they shouldn't dress me like that. Throughout my early life there was a general atmosphere of tolerance and acceptance that I believe helped create the open mindset that would serve me well later on. I'm fortunate in that, while my dressing was a point of confusion at various times, it has never been a source of shame or guilt for me or the loved ones I've made aware of it. The idea that any of this is somehow inherently wicked or wrong was never instilled in me, and I suppose those early days of freely being put in girl clothes for fun helped take the curse off it early on.

I only ever remember being told once in my life by my mother that I shouldn't be doing something that she saw as effeminate. This was a little bit later on, shortly before I hit puberty. As with anybody from my generation, I was bowled over by the movie *Who Framed Roger Rabbit*. The over-the-top character of Jessica Rabbit in particular was a source of some awe for me. At that young age I couldn't really nail down my interest in her but I knew it was there. I had a certain fascination in particular with the power she had over so many of the other characters. It was a different kind of power than I'd seen before. She wasn't pushy, she didn't twist anybody's arm, and she wasn't physically confronting people, yet she would walk into a room and clearly have all the power. I suppose I'd seen a few cartoons or movies where women used their feminine wiles on men, but it was never like this. This was weaponized sensuality, and even prior to puberty I was picking up on it. That might have been the closest I ever had to a Fay Wray Moment, but it's only in hindsight that I can spot it. At the time it was just a movie I liked.

Anyway, as an only child of a working, single mother I spent a good chunk of my free time watching movies. We didn't receive television channels—my mother hated TV and as a parent now myself I can understand why—but we had a VCR and a pretty decent library of VHS tapes. Given how much free time I had, I tended to watch the movies I enjoyed over and over again. As I started to memorize them I was less likely to just sit there and watch them; instead, I would act out the parts of my favorite characters while the movie was playing. It was in this context that my mother saw me once trying to walk with the exaggerated hip sway that I saw Jessica Rabbit doing.

This is the only time I ever remember her telling me I shouldn't do something like that. I was a fairly trusting child and I didn't ask the reason why I shouldn't be doing it, probably to her great relief. I know now that her motivation was to try to protect me from doing things that might get me bullied or even beaten up by other kids as opposed to actually trying to stop a behavior because she thought it was any kind of problem in and of itself. It's one of those moments that didn't mean much to me at the time, but looking back on it now it was probably significant. It set the stage for the general operating principal of my life when it comes to balancing my dressing with everything else: I don't really care what people think about all of this, but at the same time I have to consider the ability of people to make my life difficult if they don't like what I'm doing. For instance, my job has a very liberal dress code, at least on paper. Very little is regulated or restricted, so technically I could go in wearing a skirt and blouse with 4-inch heels and not break any rules. However, I don't do that because I know how uncomfortable those around me could make my day-to-day life if I started presenting feminine in the office. If I was ever planning to fully transition to daily life as a woman that would be one thing, but since that's not the path that I'm on it's a burden I feel is not worth it.

This is as good a place as any to point out that I've never really taken a deep psychological look at my dressing or tried to break down the precise roots of *why* I actually do it. I've never tried to work out with a therapist all of the ins and outs of Vera. I've talked with therapists about her and my existence as her, of course, but she was never a "problem" to be figured out or a behavior I felt I needed to know the origins of. Honestly, having simply accepted Vera as a part of who I am, it doesn't really make any difference to me where she comes from in terms of psychoanalysis or anything like that. I'm sure there are shrinks out there who would cite things like the lack of a strong father figure, spending more of my early years around girls than around boys, etc. And that all may be true. Regardless, I still don't care. I don't care why I have this part of me any more than I care why I'm right-handed or why I prefer my fruits to be under-ripe. There's a reason for all of these things I'm sure, but knowing the reason doesn't change anything about how I'll live my life. Some people feel paralyzed if they don't understand the reason for certain thoughts or behaviors they have. I've just never been that way.

FIRST EXPERIMENTS

While those very early times of me in girly clothes that I mentioned don't register as anything more than very dim memories of playing dress up, things started to take shape as I was going into puberty. Now, I don't know what it was that actually sparked the initial idea of putting on "girl clothes." It could have just been boredom for all I remember. That might not even be far off since I'm pretty sure I started with jewelry like rings and necklaces. But in any case, that was the age when the inclination started to manifest distinctly from within myself, as opposed to being part of dress up play with other kids. Due largely to a lack of other options, that experimentation with female attire started with my mother's clothes. I would put on what were admittedly ill-fitting dresses or bras and look at myself in the mirror. I may have even tucked my genitals back. I honestly can't remember. What I do remember is looking at these clothes on my young, hairless body in the mirror and trying to move the way I saw the women in certain films move. You see, my mother didn't do much to shield me from nudity; she was always more concerned with violence. So as long as nudity wasn't part of an actual sex scene, I could watch things like *Trading Places* (with several topless scenes featuring Jamie Lee Curtis) or *Dragnet* (which has a scene set in a strip club). These and similar scenes were my mental reference point for moving in a feminine fashion.

At first I was focusing on my body from the neck down, mentally cutting out my head and imagining that I was watching a girl dancing and moving around in front of me. I don't know when the transition came that I started to actually see myself as the girl in the mirror instead of think of her as a separate person. In my memory it wasn't like a light being switched on. It was something that came on gradually as I became more comfortable moving around in the clothes and jewelry that I was wearing. But just as I was starting to get a feel for all of this and finding that it filled some kind of urge, I had to stop.

When I was in my early teens my mother met (and eventually married) a man with kids of his own, four of whom were still in school. When he moved into the house it meant that not only was there an adult male in my life where there had not been one before, but there were also numerous step-siblings suddenly in and out of the house. I was fortunate in that I never had to give up having my own room, but my level of privacy was cut substantially. Before, I would often have the entire house to myself, as I was home from school several hours before my mother was out of her job. Now the house was almost never empty, and even my room felt less secure than it had previously. I never had any shame or fear about what I was doing, but I still knew enough to recognize that it was something private and personal, if for no other reason that it involved having to take clothes off and on. So with my privacy so drastically slashed I pretty much just stopped dressing feminine altogether.

Stopping almost completely like I did was also compounded by the fact that the man my mother brought into my life never felt right to me. Even in the early days I was never able to connect with him. Initially, this was due to his attitude towards his own children (and towards myself) which just didn't jive with how I'd been raised or how I believed that parents and children should act towards each other. Essentially he was a "because I said so" type parent, whereas my mother had always made me feel like I had a voice in any decision that directly affected me, even if I didn't really have the final say. She always made me feel that I was being heard. By contrast, my step-father's belief that I wasn't yet an adult and therefore my opinion didn't count for anything put me at odds with him from the start. But even beyond different parenting styles I just never felt comfortable with him, and I never felt like I could trust him with my private business. This feeling of unease was eventually validated over time as he revealed himself to be a bully and a bigot. And neither of these are terms that I toss out lightly.

It took a few years before he began to openly express his intolerant views around me and my mother (which included the assertion that "homosexuality is an abomination on the earth"). Not all of his children bought into this, but some did (one in particular had no issue casually tossing out the term "fucking faggots" and similar phrases) and that only made things more awkward for me. I didn't really have a sense of my sexual preferences at that point, but I knew even being in a questioning state was going to result in ridicule at the very least. The worst thing was that it indirectly cut me off from my mother. While I wouldn't trust this man with my secrets, I did still trust my mother. However, I knew that she didn't see in him what I saw, not in those earlier days anyway. And because she thought better of him than I did, I feared that anything I shared with her would eventually be told to him as well, because she trusted him. So I kept to myself more than ever before.

I wish I could say that just keeping my head down got me through things, but it barely did. My step-father was a relentless bully, although he would label it as "joking" or "teasing." Whatever he chose to call it, it was always mean-spirited, intending to belittle my own self-worth, and he never relented no matter how much I said it bothered me. From his perspective it was my fault for not being able to take a joke and for having a thin skin. And I realize even as I write this that many dressers had it much worse than me. He never physically abused me. He was rarely outright aggressive in his belittling. It was simply done over time as a persistent emotional jab. And it made me hate: hate him, hate how powerless it made me feel, and even hate myself at one point. And much like "bully" and "bigot," I want to stress that "hate" is also not a word I use lightly.

My mother did eventually divorce this man, but that did not come about until after I'd moved out of the house. By then the major damage had been done and left me feeling isolated. I want to be clear that I have no ill will against my mother for any of this. She is a wonderful person who is inclined to believe the best of people. I would never call her naïve but I sense that, for a time, it was hard for her to believe that the man she'd fallen in love with had this other side to him that would never change. Since then I myself have gone through the experience of falling in love with someone who was equally as wrong for me. And I also didn't want to admit that. Additionally, in the years since, I've found out that my mother did know that he was not somebody she needed in her life much earlier than I'd suspected. But she stayed married to him until his kids completed high school because they were on her insurance (he was self-employed) and she cared too much about them to leave them in a lurch like that. Knowing all this, I don't begrudge that she tried to make it work with him and then stuck around for a few more years even when she knew it had to end.

I can't say that dressing or exploring my femininity was entirely swept away in the wake of my step-father's arrival and the associated privacy loss, but it dwindled to a drip feed. When we moved into a bigger house to accommodate the larger family my privacy felt slightly restored, thanks in part to a lock on my bedroom door. At that point I was free to do things in my room that I wouldn't do in places where my step-family were liable to see, things like lip syncing and dancing to songs by female singers. Again, I wasn't really imagining myself as female at this point, at least not on a conscious level. It was just something that I did for fun that I knew others in the house wouldn't understand or would make fun of. I didn't think too much about the fact that I favored female pop stars at the time. (That's something that hasn't changed as I've become an adult.)

I suppose the fact that I just did these things without an agenda or clear cause is part of how I've ultimately come to terms with this side of myself. As I said earlier, it just is. I don't dress and act as a woman for attention or sexual kicks. I do it because there are times that it feels natural to me, just like dancing to songs sung by women singers did in high school—it's not something I did all the time, but when the mood hit I went with it. Like how moving my hips in a feminine fashion could just feel like the right thing to do sometimes. Or how I tend to gravitate towards female playable characters in video games if they are available

(Cammy was my go-to character in *Street Fighter 2: Championship Edition* and the Rogue was my favorite *Diablo* class). Dressing has become very much the same thing for me now. I don't feel the need to do it all the time, but when I want to do it I know that I'm free to.

THE COLLEGE YEARS

College is where things started really coming together. Well, maybe not right off the bat. My first year of college was both an enlightening and floundering experience. Due to a very poor bit of reasoning on my part, I found myself at a business college intending to major in accounting. My thinking at the time was that even though my passions were on the artsy side (acting, writing, etc.) having a degree in those things doesn't really increase your odds of "making it" in those areas. So instead I opted to major in my backup plan in case the things I really cared about didn't pan out. In hindsight, this was a horrible idea—I only lasted a year at the business college. Not because of the work itself. It was the environment. I quickly realized I couldn't stand about 95% of the student population. I was surrounded by people in designer clothes, talking on cell phones (this was well before they became a standard item and instead were only the playthings of the rich and self-important), and with vanity plates on the cars their parents had bought for them. They came from money and were getting into business in order to remain rich. Their idea of what was a worthwhile pursuit was almost strictly tied to money. I know that these are all generalizations, but it was simply the environment of the school as a whole. I realized that if this was representative of the people I'd be working with in this field then I needed to rethink where I was and quickly.

That first year in the wrong school did have its uses, however; it proved to be an enlightening social experience. I quickly found the other people who didn't really fit in either. They all were in Alpha Psi Omega, the theater frat (go figure). Finding these people who shared my interests and passions helped me come out of my shell a bit.

My dressing didn't really come back in full during that first year of college, but I was comfortable enough with the friends I had that I was able to play with my more effeminate tendencies. I wasn't ashamed to strike a girly pose for a picture at a party, or throw on a boa from the prop room if it felt right. So in many ways it was rebuilding the foundation that had been neglected in high school, finding that comfort and the freedom to just do what felt good.

At an Alpha Psi Omega party. Probably an early indicator of my future dressing.

Oddly enough, my social life would have to dwindle somewhat before dressing really came back into my life with true prominence. For my second year of college I changed schools and majors to ones that were much more suited to me. The college also happened to be a little closer to home. However, in a strange way, that actually crippled my social life. When I was at the business school it was such a bad fit and people like myself (I mean misfits in general, not people questioning gender issues specifically) were so few that we all found each other and held on for dear life. In my new school where like-minded folks were much more abundant, there wasn't the inherent need to congregate together in order to survive. I've never been great at reaching out to people I don't know. I do much better when circumstance presents me with potential friends, as it had the year before and throughout high school, thanks to things like the drama club. In those situations I had an organization where the same people would congregate at regular intervals and I didn't have to actively engage much outside of that in order to have friends. Now it was harder and circumstance wasn't on my side any longer. So despite attending a larger school with more people like myself, I actually ended up more isolated than I was that first year when I was at the wrong school in the wrong major. And that's where online chat came in.

Folks my age will remember the early 2000s as the heyday of AIM and Yahoo messenger, and if I was in my dorm (which I usually was) then I was almost constantly on both of them. I'd actually experimented with online chat for some time back when we'd first gotten an Internet-capable computer at home (I would have been 13 or so). However, the pains of a dial-up connection meant I never really got into chatting online. I do remember going into more than a few chat rooms in my early teens and pretending I was a girl. I didn't think much of it. At the time it was for shits and giggles, and it was actually a bit of a cliché observation that all the women in the lesbian chat room were men. It was a bit of self-deception that, along with most of my dressing activities, dropped off during high school when my privacy was curtailed.

In my new college I quickly found myself hopping around Yahoo chat rooms rather regularly. At the time Yahoo was where you could find virtually everything because users had the ability to create their own publicly-searchable chats on any topic they wanted. This is something that was done away with some years later (too many morally- and legally-questionable topics were created, and Yahoo was held accountable in the public eye for what went on in them). At the time, however, it meant that if you could imagine it then there was a chat room for it somewhere. This was ideal for someone trying to find himself, or I suppose "herself" in this case.

I found myself spending more time in these chat rooms, and on the computer in general, than I'd care to admit. That first year at my second college I didn't have a webcam, but I would send scanned pictures of myself to fellow chatters from time to time. And the reactions I got from some of the people I shared my picture with rekindled an interest in dressing more actively.

You see, the high school I attended had a dress code that included a hair length restriction for men. That meant that once I was out of high school one of the first things I did was grow my hair out. It wasn't with any intention of trying to look "girly", it was just something I hadn't been given the chance to do before. I remember there was one man I chatted with online who saw my picture and asked me flat out if I ever dressed as a girl. Since it wasn't something I was active with at the time I told him "no." It was easier than going into the "well I used to but not anymore" history of everything. He commented that it was a shame and that I'd be gorgeous.

This compliment really got the wheels turning in a completely conscious way for the first time. The idea had been planted that I could actually be an attractive woman, an idea that made the entire thing much more appealing. Because, if I'm being completely honest, there's an ego component in all of this for me, which is part of why I didn't really do the halfway or mixed gender dressing that some folks go for. It wasn't enough for me to just put on a skirt or a blouse. I can't just slip on a pair of pantyhose and feel appropriately feminine. I have to go all the way: makeup, hair, heels, shaved body hair, and breast forms all have to be in place before I can feel truly feminine. Even now it's important for me that I look good, though my definition of what that means has continued to evolve.

I do want to make the distinction between looking good or looking feminine and actually passing for female. I came to accept some time ago that I will likely never be able to truly pass myself off as a woman (my height, for one thing, is usually a serious clue that I can't hide). So I don't worry about passing or fooling people into thinking I was female at birth. Instead, I've focused on looking pretty. I've come to believe quite firmly that looking beautiful and feminine is not the same as being passable. They're related, of course, but one does not require the other. Sure, I may be a man in a dress and maybe people can tell that, but I look *damn* good. The idea of being attractive is very important to me when I dress. I'm probably not supposed to admit that because it's superficial and self-involved. But it's also just how I am, and it'd be dishonest of me to claim otherwise. I have no doubt that more than a few readers right now have the image of Buffalo Bill in *Silence of the Lambs* popping into their heads. You know, the part where he tucks his junk, looks in the mirror and says, "Would you fuck me? I'd fuck me." And while I'm loath to be compared to a cinematic serial killer, there's more than a little grain of truth in that moment for me. In that sentiment at least. Not the whole "I want to literally wear a woman's skin" thing.

So that one little online interaction where it was suggested that I could be beautiful relit the fire that had been gently smoldering underneath the surface for years. I found myself wearing nail polish on a semi-regular basis, even to classes. I was going into cross dressing-themed chats (rather than just pretending I was a "real" girl) and looking for images and video of dressers, trying to get a sense of what it would be like to explore this further. Of course, this being the Internet, everything was heavily skewed towards the sexual and pornographic, something that would cause some questioning for me further down the line. But in many ways this is where thoughts of dressing started to become more frequent and prominent for me. I can recognize the foundations being laid before this, but this was the point when I started to flat out imagine presenting as female, for myself and for others.

CHAPTER TWO

WHAT'S IN A NAME?

Let's take a break from my own history and talk a little bit about something that I think many dressers tend to either struggle with or just not put enough thought into: what to call themselves when they get dressed up. Choosing a feminine name seems like such an easy thing. Just pick one and go with it. But it never works out quite that easily.

Many names can carry certain implications as to the kind of woman who would have them. So many dressers who either have an inherently sexual interest in dressing are quick to jump onto what I tend to think of as porn or stripper names. Trixie, Candy, and Roxie would be go-to examples, but really most two syllable names ending in "y," "i," or "ie" have the same vibe (Barbie, Kimmy, Nikki, etc.). These names sound more inherently girly, which is the reason for their appeal to many dressers. But they also carry some pretty immediate impressions about the girls who have them. There's an expectation that women with names like these (especially if they've chosen the name for themselves) are going to be more outwardly sexual, or even flat out easy to get into bed.

I'm not saying that this is the reality, and I'm not making any statement about anyone who has any of these names or ones like them. But we need to be realistic about the baggage these names carry, regardless of whether that baggage is fair or not. I'm also not saying that these are names to be avoided. Frankly, some dressers wish to be thought of in the sexual terms that come with these kinds of names, and there's nothing wrong with that. However, many dressers would benefit from thinking about the implied sexual baggage some names carry before starting to use them.

Of course, there's no reason to keep using a name that you ultimately decide doesn't suit you. In my early days of online chatting I changed names at least half a dozen times, sometimes on little more than a whim. I started with a common option: the feminized version of my masculine name. Ultimately I had to abandon this one due to circumstances outside of my control. My girlfriend, and eventual wife, had a sister whose name happened to match the feminized version of my male name. While she'd been supportive from the start with regards to my dressing (we'll go more into this later), me going by the same name as her sister weirded her out, and I don't blame her one bit.

In hindsight it was for the best anyway, given where dressing would settle into my life later on. The reason that I say that is because I think choosing the feminine version of your masculine name (Michael to Michelle, Paul to Paula, Nicolas to Nicole, etc.) blurs the lines between living as a man and living as a woman a little bit. For those who decide to transition to something more full-time or otherwise have a feminine existence more fully integrated into their day-to-day living that isn't really an issue. It can even ease the transition for some. But for myself, I went through a very long stretch of time where I found it best to keep my feminine and masculine lives fairly separate from each other in terms of how I live my daily life. That's something I'll talk more about later on (including how it changed), but for about a decade it helped me mentally come to terms with all of this to have a clear separation of male and female modes. Having clearly separate and distinct names kept the line firm and for a decent chunk of time I needed that.

Coming back to changing names, it was an easy thing when I was just an online dresser. All I had to do was make a new chat ID and I was good to go. However, once I was ready to start actually going out in public dressed as a woman I decided that it was time to pick a name and stick with it. Oddly enough, I settled on one that wasn't any of the names I'd been using online up to that point. When I actually think about it, Vera is a strange choice. It's an old-fashioned name and that implication is not reflective of my sense of style or demeanor. Though since it is a bit of an out-of-date name that meant there were far less dressers using it, which ended up as a nice bonus.

The way I came up with the name was to literally sit down and start writing up a list of possibilities. I was in my early 20s at the time. I consulted my girlfriend as to which ones she liked and we both found ourselves gravitating towards Vera. The reason that name was on the list in the first place was because of my high school years of listening endlessly to the Pink Floyd album *The Wall*. On it there is a song titled "Vera" about the World War II era singer and actress Vera Lynn. I actually used Lynn as a middle name for a while, though I've kind of moved on from it. It's still there but I don't put it front and center like I once did.

The other reason I gravitated to Vera was knowing that its written and spoken resemblance to the word "very" meant it had word play potential depending on the last name I chose. I knew by that point I wanted to at least dip my toes into drag performance, so I tried to come up with a name that was playful enough to work as a stage name but wasn't so over the top that it couldn't be used day to day. Wylde, of course, is nothing more than a pretentious spelling of "wild." So in a loose play on "very wild" I became Vera Wylde, and have been happy with it ever since.

FIRST PURCHASES

This desire to start exploring the idea of dressing up as a girl and, more importantly to me at the time, allowing people to see it over the Internet, brought about that most dreaded of experiences: shopping for feminine clothing. This is something that most dressers, especially those just starting out or still in the closet, have a great deal of fear about. I know I had my share. It wasn't so much that I worried about the workers in the store knowing I was buying for these things for myself, as in general I maintained an "it's not any of your business" attitude even back then. However, this is when the logistics of where I lived worked against me.

Growing up and living in a relatively small town meant that it was much more likely that I could run into somebody who'd sold me girly clothes while I was out in public. Or that someone who already knew me might be in the store and see me buying the clothes in the first place. That was something that did worry me. I knew this was still something I was working out for myself. I figured once I got a handle on it I probably wouldn't care anymore (which has turned out to be the case) but back then I knew this was still very early and I didn't want it to follow me in case I decided to stop dressing.

I'd bought nail polish before and thought nothing of it, but boys with nail polish were not especially scandalous, even back then. Buying actual girl clothes was another thing altogether (I wouldn't dip into makeup for a while). At this point I wanted stuff that actually fit me as best as I could manage, and I wanted to be able to take it back to college with me. This meant that "borrowing" anything from the women in my life (mother, girlfriend, etc.) was out of the question. There was also the fact that snatching clothes in that manner increased the chances of being caught, something I wasn't ready for. I was going to have to get my own stuff.

I remember very distinctly the first garment I ever bought for myself. It was a green thong. It seems silly now in hindsight, with what I've since learned about which garments work for a dresser and which ones don't. I still have it, even though I don't wear it anymore, and indeed haven't for years. It never fit quite right to be honest, but I wouldn't dream of getting rid of it. It marks the beginning of an era in a way. The store I bought it from was a short-lived adult store that set up shop in my home town shortly after I started college. Like many adult stores it carried a mix of things: videos, magazines, adult toys, and a smattering of goofily sexy clothing items like crotchless teddies and skimpy nurse outfits. The thong was one of these kinds of items. Given the nature of this place, and the fact that this type of business depended on discretion, I knew that I could safely purchase something here and nobody would say anything. If I'd had more money to spend I probably would have gotten a full outfit, but being a college student with a part-time job meant most of my income was blown on gas to simply get myself around.

I've occasionally had people ask me what first items they should buy for themselves, and I've had to tell them that they're the only ones who would know. My inclination is to say that you should buy whatever article of clothing you find yourself most drawn to. Maybe it's a dress, or stockings, or a pair of panties that you could wear under everyday clothes (i.e. *not* that thong). If you're tight on cash or are having a hard time selecting just one thing, I suppose I'd say go for a bra or an inexpensive dress. The reason I recommend these is because they're items of clothing that don't have a direct masculine analog so they'll have a uniquely feminine feel to them. In the case of the bra there's a bonus because you can stuff it and then start to get a sense of yourself with a more feminine silhouette. Take a quick measurement of your chest with a tape measure (the loose sewing kind, not the stiff carpenter's kind). Wrap it all the way around, keeping it lined up across your nipples. That'll give you a rough measurement for a bra that is close enough for a first purchase and you can go with whatever cup size you feel like.

As I said, that first thong that I bought never really fit particularly well. The reason for this is obvious in hindsight: I guessed at the size and didn't try it on before buying it. I would learn later on down the road that standard thongs aren't a great item if you're trying to actually dress to go out anyway. They do a poor job of containing the male genitals and don't allow for a proper tuck. That said, it was still a very important first step for me, and that's why I keep it even today.

THE ONLINE LIFE

As I mentioned earlier, I started getting heavily into online chats while I was in college, and that's something that stayed true pretty much right up until I started going out in public. While I've never abandoned the Internet, I did eventually give up chat rooms for more casual social media like Myspace, to be followed later by Facebook, Twitter, YouTube, Snapchat, and the like. These sites and tools allowed me to keep my online presence and the empowerment I felt from having it, without demanding huge chunks of my time the way that chat rooms had. Now I can just pop on, see what's happening, do a quick update, answer a message or two, and pop off again. This suits my adult life very well.

By contrast, those early days in chat rooms were a massive time sink. I would lose entire nights of sleep in what felt like the blink of an eye, which naturally didn't do my academic life any favors. I hesitate to call it an addiction, but I have to admit that it had that similar pattern. I was losing hours of time chasing what amounted to only minutes of actual enjoyment and affirmation. If I'd ever taken a closer look at how much time I was losing versus what I was getting out of it I probably would have cut back. The problem was at that point I didn't know how else to get the positive reinforcement that I wanted in regards to my dressing. I didn't know how else to feel feminine other than to try to appeal to the people in those chat rooms. At the time, I didn't really have anyone in real life to help me get a handle on this side of myself, and I'm not sure I would have been ready to make that leap even if I found somebody. Eventually my girlfriend would find out about my dressing. Though she was supportive, she wouldn't become an active part of my figuring this all out until a bit later (which I will talk about, don't worry). And even then it took some time before I properly broke away from the chat rooms. Looking back I can see that the lost time in chats was all part of the process of finding myself, but for a while it was time that I wished I could have back.

Part of the problem with an online existence, especially when it comes to dressing, is that the supposed anonymity of the Internet encourages more extreme behavior than one would encounter or engage in while out in the real world. The idea that nobody knows what we're doing makes it easier to for us to let ourselves believe there aren't serious consequences to it. This makes it very easy for dressers who are just starting to explore all of this to fall under the influence of those who see them only as sex objects. The best way to feel feminine is to be treated like you are; unfortunately, the easiest way to get that is to appeal to the people who will sexualize you in a feminine fashion. Even if I went into a cross dressing chat room that wasn't meant to be explicitly sexual, it would only be a matter of time before I'd be sent some private message asking me very sexual questions or hoping to view me performing sexual acts. Even later on when I moved away from chats and was putting the fact that I was in a relationship (and later, that I was married) front and center in my profiles on all my social media accounts, I would still get solicited by men. Part of the problem is that most of these men had leapt to the conclusion that I was in some way submissive, and they assumed if they showed enough force they could dominate me into doing what they wanted. And they did this because sometimes it works. As I mentioned, so many of us are chasing that affirmation of our femininity and a dominant male sexualizing us can become a very tempting thing if we're not getting what we need elsewhere.

Now, I do need to acknowledge that there are many dressers for whom the sexual aspects are truly the appeal of cross dressing. It's also true that many of those same people do fall on the submissive side of things. And I need to be absolutely clear that there isn't a single thing wrong with that. I would never want to imply that those who want and desire sexual experience as part of their dressing are doing something they shouldn't be. If it makes you truly happy, then it's the right thing for you. However, it's also an easy trap to fall into for those who aren't in this strictly for sex. For those who simply want to be treated like a woman, and not necessarily used sexually as a feminized plaything, the ease of online reinforcement can lead to a great deal of confusion. You may not want to be seen as a sex object, but kowtowing to the people who see you this way grants an immediate validation of your feminine self. The need for this validation can lead to hasty decisions and deep regrets. At best, it's confusing for those who are still figuring themselves out and trying to find how all of this fits into their lives. It often contributes to a cycle that I've seen so many dressers fall into: going further than one is comfortable with, swearing off dressing, and purging one's feminine wardrobe, only to have the need to dress resurface and start the cycle again. I've seen it time and time again, and been told about such cycles by more dressers than I can count. While I never had a purge cycle myself, I went through the same kind of confusion that spawns that behavior.

The other thing about the perceived anonymity of the Internet is that it leads to quite a bit of general flakiness. There's the obvious flakiness of people who will be chatting with you and then they just vanish without explanation. This can be extremely deflating when it happens, but the anonymity of the Internet also encourages us as dressers to act in fickle ways as well. If we feel that we've taken things in a direction we don't like, we change our user IDs and just start over. There's nothing inherently wrong with doing this from time to time as needed but, speaking personally, when I was big into chat rooms it was so easy that it was another factor which encouraged people to take things too far and then just hit the reset button by creating a new profile. No real consequences and no lessons learned. It felt like it was easy to run away and it makes risky or exposing behavior feel safer than it should.

These days the myth of Internet anonymity has been largely exposed for the lie that it is. Most people seem to understand that if they put their faces out there (even in wigs and makeup) they can be identified. More importantly, once your image is on the Internet you can't take it back. Of course, that doesn't stop people, especially younger people who don't appreciate the long-term impact of their actions, from living very exposed online lives. I've also seen this happen with those who are closeted in their personal lives.

Sometimes it seems that the more one is repressed at home the more that person wants to expose it all to supposed strangers, just as a means of release. Sadly, my observation is that this is more likely to lead to that cycle of guilt, purging, and resurgence.

Online communities, chat rooms, and social media can be wonderful outlets for those just starting to explore cross dressing, so long as they're approached with a degree of caution. If you're living in a smaller community or just aren't yet ready to go out to real-life events, it can give you a sense of belonging that is essential to coming to terms with whatever cross dressing is to you. However, these online tools are also dangerous in terms of the behavior and the level of exposure that they encourage. You should avoid putting anything out there on the Internet that you aren't ok with people discovering. Given the heat of the moment and the thrill of positive reinforcement, that's often easier said than done, but it's the goal to keep in mind regardless. No matter how much you may think you can trust the person on the other end of a web chat you must remember that *anything* you do, say, or show online can come back to haunt you. You may delete photos you put up, but somebody else could have saved them. It's possible that somebody watching your webcam display recorded it. In the end, a healthy degree of paranoia and presumption that anything you put out there will eventually be found and linked to you is to your benefit.

CHAPTER THREE

BEING DISCOVERED

Most dressers start experimenting on their own and it quickly becomes a very private activity. This is pretty much the case regardless of the reason for dressing, whether it's sexual in nature, the start of a more complete gender transition, or simply an exercise in gender exploration. Granted, I had a bit of an online presence starting in college, but I still felt it was a very private activity, and something that I shouldn't let people around me know about. It wasn't shame driving this need for privacy; rather, it was a desire to not complicate my life needlessly. It seemed easier to keep it to myself than to try and explain it to people, especially when I wasn't sure how large or important a part of my life this would be. If I'd known myself back then as well as I do now I probably would have been much more open about all of it from an earlier age. But when you aren't even sure about yourself, you hate to invite questions about your activities that you can't really answer.

However, hiding something you're doing naturally leads to the fear of discovery, a fear that all closeted dressers have. Sometimes that fear comes from knowing that certain people in our lives won't accept us. That was certainly the case with my step-father. Most of the time, however, what it comes down to is a fear of the unknown: not knowing how people will react and being afraid to find out. There's the fear of being judged, of being looked down on, of rejection, or of the people in your life simply not understanding you. In regards to being discovered, I know that I'm one of the lucky ones. I could have been caught at any number of points in my life. It could have been by my mother when I was first starting out, by my roommates when I started up again in college, or the one that frightened me the most: being caught by any member of my step-family. Thankfully, none of these things came to pass.

During my third year of college I managed to get a single room with no roommate. The privacy was something I welcomed greatly, though in truth it probably wasn't a great thing for me at that point. I effectively became a shut-in: always in my room and always on my computer. I now recognize I needed to be forced to interact with others at that point in my life, and having a roommate the year before had filled that need. Now, isolation just begat more isolation. In terms of my dressing, it did mean I could experiment more and do it more brazenly in the privacy of my own room. (This was the point when I even tried shaving my legs for the first time.)

That's not to say that I literally never left my room. I still went to a few classes (though not as many or as often as I should have) and to my part-time job at a local bookstore. I also started seeing Laura, the woman who would eventually become my wife of 11 years. We met online. She attended a college about an hour's drive from me, and knew some people I had gone to high school with. We chatted online for a bit before deciding to meet in person. On our first date we talked, grabbed some food, and went to a movie. It was nice, and it was definitely more involved than any relationship I'd had for a couple of years; college was filled with more hook-ups than I'd care to count.

Laura and I started seeing each other regularly after that. Due to the distance between our respective schools, often one of us would spend the night with the other. Being a young male living in a single room, it should go without saying that my room was a bit of a disaster area. One day when she came over I had a morning shift at work, which meant she was effectively on her own for a bit. So she made the ambitious decision to try and tidy up my room.

When I came back to the room Laura confronted me with a pair of white pantyhose. She demanded to know whose they were and was clearly upset by her discovery. Figuring that I had nothing to lose at that point, I rather sheepishly admitted to her that they were, in fact, mine. She paused and absorbed this notion for a few seconds before saying, "Oh. Well, that's ok then."

It was like a weight had been lifted off my shoulders. I'd been found out and it wasn't the end of the world. The truth had actually diffused a tense situation. We didn't talk about it directly for a long time after that. Not because we were avoiding the subject but because she seemed to just get it. She accepted that this was part of me and even encouraged it. (On one occasion not long after the discovery of the pantyhose she did my hair in a French braid and put me in a dress, largely because she was bored.) She never made fun of me for it, never made me feel guilty about it, and actually helped me a great deal in finding a place for all of this in my life.

I wish I could say that we lived happily ever after, but sadly we would eventually split, though I want to emphasize that it was not because of my dressing habits. Laura was only ever supportive about this aspect of my life and remains so. She was invaluable in my own journey of self-acceptance, and she remains my best friend.

From talking with many other dressers online I know how uniquely fortunate I was in my one experience of being "caught" as a cross dresser. I wish I could say that all our fears of what could go wrong have no real foundation in truth, but I know that's not the case. So many have told me horror stories about being caught by unaccepting family members, friends who then abandoned them, or significant others who felt betrayed such a big secret was kept from them. The simple truth is that being caught is almost never a positive experience. I just got lucky.

FIRST TIME OUT IN PUBLIC

My very first time ever going out in public in a dress was with Laura before we were married. We were not actually dating at the time. It was during a period we'd broken off the romantic relationship but were still friends (which isn't far off from how things are now, come to think of it). Before ever meeting me she'd regularly gone to the midnight showings of *The Rocky Horror Picture Show* in Harvard Square. (Funny how that movie keeps cropping up, isn't it?) This was an experience she wanted to share with me.

I'd been introduced to *The Rocky Horror Picture Show* at the age of 13, and by my mother of all people. She just thought it was something I'd enjoy, and I did immensely. I thought the music was amazing and I was naturally mesmerized by

Tim Curry, as well as Riff Raff, played by Richard O'Brien. While I was aware of the existence of midnight showings, my experience with the film before this outing had always been with home viewings by myself. I'd never lived in an area where there were midnight showings, though I did have a general idea of what went on during them. So I was more than ready to head down to the show. Part of the deal, however, was that Laura wanted to do my makeup and loan me a dress and boots to wear. She'd already discovered my dressing tendencies by that point and didn't exactly have to twist my arm. The resulting night is one of my strongest and most detailed memories.

The trip was a bit of an event unto itself, as it wasn't exactly a short drive down. Being college students, we weren't swimming in disposable income, so we had just enough money to pay for gas and to get into the show. This meant scrounging for non-essentials, like food. On the way down we stopped at a mall and did a quick spin around the food court, grabbing whatever free samples were being handed out to keep us going (thank you Panda Express). We arrived at Harvard Square with time to spare but nothing to do. Since the food court samples didn't exactly fill us up we bummed change from strangers until we had enough for a snack bag of Fritos and M&M's. (We opted for the peanut M&M's, figuring those would be more filling.)

Finally it was time for Laura to do my makeup. This she did in the car, the closest thing to a private location we had. It wasn't particularly elaborate makeup; she just did my eyes and lips. She didn't do anything about my hair because I'd grown it out to shoulder length at that point. Then came the time for me to squeeze into the black vinyl dress and knee-high boots. The dress was actually a good fit, owing to how clingy and stretchy it was by design. I've used it quite a bit since, and still have it as of this writing. It was a rather short dress, barely covering the top of my thighs. The boots were a little tougher on me, as my feet were larger than hers. I was able to squeeze into them, though just barely, and my feet were quite sore by the end of the evening. I topped off the outfit with a collar and a bit of finger armor I'd picked up at a Hot Topic.

Stepping out of the car and into the open air was a strange and thrilling experience. I probably couldn't have done it without her there to tell me that I looked hot and, more importantly, to hold my hand as we approached the theater. The air hitting my thighs was probably the thing that felt the strangest. I wore shorts on occasion, but never anything that was shorter than just above the knee. So this part of my body had never really been exposed before, and there was something both exciting and frightening about that.

There were some looks, some double takes, and a few whispers from people we passed getting to the theater. But she held my hand and smiled at me and I knew that everything was going to be ok.

First time in public, waiting in line to get into The Rocky
Horror Picture Show.

Once we were in line to get into the show I didn't feel so out
of place. Not many were as done-up for the show as I was,
but they certainly weren't judging me. Most smiled; some
seemed impressed. A few even contested my claim that it
was my first time at the midnight showing. They believed
that if I was getting this decked out I must do it all the time,
which was a nice boost to my confidence.

Once inside the theater my being dressed took a backseat to
the experience of a midnight showing of *Rocky Horror*. If
you've never been to one I highly recommend it, regardless
of whether you have cross dressing proclivities or not. But
be sure you already know the movie fairly well, because
between the antics of the live performers going on in front
of the screen and the callbacks being hollered by the
audience you aren't actually going to see much of the movie.

After the show we went back to the car and drove back north, as if it was just another typical night out. That night is still one of my favorite memories. Laura went to great lengths to not only make me look good and make me feel confident in how I appeared but also to make it all feel normal. She never made me feel like what I was doing was weird, which was what I needed more than anything else.

FIRST TIME MODELING

Even before I started going out dressed in public on a more regular basis, I set about trying to find photographers to work with. I wasn't yet confident that I would be able to convincingly pass as a woman walking down the street (a hang up that I'd just eventually get over), but I knew that I could be good enough to get some great shots if paired with somebody who knew what they were doing. This was after college and it's the point where Craigslist entered the picture.

I honestly don't know how useful Craigslist is anymore in regards to finding legitimate modeling work, or at least "time for print" modeling (which is where the model is "paid" with copies of the pictures to use as they see fit). I haven't bothered with Craigslist for a while now, but much of the modeling work available at the time skewed towards the pornographic, something that appears to have gotten worse from what I can discern. Those looking to get into modeling these days would likely do better with sites like Model Mayhem or just old fashioned in-person networking. However, at the time there were plenty of postings on the site that panned out as legitimate, especially in larger cities like Boston, which was where I was living when I had my first shoots taken.

For those who are looking for time for print work, a good place to consider making your availability known is any college with a photography program. Students are always after models who won't charge for their time, and you'll get copies of the pictures at the end. Just be aware of the general attitudes of the college before trying this, as some are more liberally-minded than others. But as long as it's not a religiously-based school then odds are there are at least a few photography students who will be interested in the challenge of shooting an atypical model, such as a dresser or trans individual.

Getting back to my time in Boston—at that point I still had hopes of somehow getting into acting (with absolutely no real plan of how to pull that off, of course, which was probably one of numerous reasons that I never became an actor). Modeling wasn't really a goal, but it seemed like the kind of experience that would be useful. And if I could come away with some good pictures of myself in dress, all the better. So I used Craigslist to find any modeling I could get, as well as open auditions for independent films and local theater. It didn't lead to much. I appeared in one student short and a film that a friend of mine made which never found distribution. My first few times modeling weren't in dress. Instead, I posed nude as a figure model, once for a class and a few times for a local artist. There was something liberating about posing nude. There was also a certain amount of safety in the fact that I was being drawn rather than photographed.

That took some of the stress out so I was able to find my footing with it. After being an art model for a few months I found a photographer who was looking for unusual models, and I thought that myself in drag might just qualify.

That first time modeling in front of a camera in a professional setting was both intimidating and thrilling. Of course I'd taken pictures of myself in the past, but they were mostly just snapshots with my webcam (which had low resolution and therefore was very forgiving about things like rough makeup work). My clothing selection at the time was limited. I had underwear and breast forms to fill out the bra, a couple of dresses, and a few scant fun items like a negligee and gloves. I barely had a handle on makeup at that point and I really didn't know how to model in a feminine manner. Mostly I didn't know what to do with my face. I felt like I could do decent work with my poses, but I just didn't know what expressions would be feminine without seeming forced.

Thankfully, none of that really mattered once I got to the shoot. What the photographer ended up doing was a perfect match for where I was at that point in my dressing. The photographer worked in black and white and he used me to experiment with heavy shadows and silhouettes. This meant that even the pictures where my face was not in shadow were forgiving of the fact that the makeup was beyond basic. The best shots didn't even have my face clearly in them. The pressure of facial expression was gone and I could just focus on holding my body in a feminine way, something I actually felt comfortable with from my time on webcam. The shots that I came away with are still some of my favorites I've ever done (I used one of them on my business cards for a long time) and they were an immense boost to my confidence. I feel like a massive ass for the fact that I long ago lost the photographer's contact information and can't give him proper credit for these photos (which is why I'm not able to use them here), but honestly I wasn't keeping track of those things back then like I do now.

FINDING A REAL-LIFE COMMUNITY

Aside from its relative ease and presumed anonymity, one of the reasons I gravitated towards chat rooms and an online dressing life was simply a lack of other options. I grew up and went to college in Vermont which, while a fairly tolerant state, is not exactly a bastion of diversity. As a result, opportunities started to open for me when I moved to Boston.

Boston was the ideal city for me at the time. It's large enough that it has almost anything you'd want from a city, yet it still feels smaller and more intimate than most big cities. You can walk through Boston Common and you don't feel the city encroaching on you the way you do with Central Park in New York City. Just the vibe of the place is more in keeping with what I'd grown up with than I've found in most other large cities I've been to. It's also where I finally found a real-life community where I could be open with my dressing.

I didn't seek out any kind of real-life group, or cross dressing support, or anything like that. Rather, I was just trying to find a job. One of the things I did while trying to find more than just temp work was go to bartending school. Following that, I started looking into the gay bars in the city. It wasn't with any agenda to be able to dress, it was just that I figured I was likely to get better tips that way (and I was right, for the record). That's how I became a barback (restocking the coolers and picking up glasses) and occasional bartender at Machine near Fenway Park.

This was really my first introduction to the real world LGBTQ+ scene, and to two very different sides of it at that. There were actually two clubs in the building where I worked. Machine was the dance club, located downstairs, and it had a stage that occasionally featured performances, including LGBTQ+-themed plays. Upstairs was Ramrod, which was a leather bar. I rarely worked in Ramrod during operating hours, though I did help stock the bar and clean up at the end of the night. Still, it was educational to be shown right off the bat that there is no single definitive LGBTQ+ experience, but rather just as many variants as there are in "straight" life.

It wasn't very long before I began working in a dress, wig, and makeup. I knew I'd be accepted doing it and the low lighting of a club made me less self-conscious about my appearance as I was still figuring out makeup.

Working at Machine was also my introduction to real-life cross dressing, more specifically drag queens. I do feel the need to specify, because while cross dressing is a very broad term, drag queen is a term used more specifically for male performers who take on a female persona when performing, and usually a highly-stylized and exaggerated persona at that. Some don't even cross dress once they're off the stage, while others I knew were actually in the process of a full transition into life as a woman. One and all, though, they were stunning. Gorgeous, glamorous, and frankly quite intimidating. I thought I could never measure up to what I was seeing, in terms of both general appearance and feminine poise.

Thankfully, not all of the queens at the club suffered from the diva mentality that is so common amongst this type of performer (an attitude I'd see much more of in New York). The ones I met in Boston were never snarky towards me; some were even welcoming despite the fact that I was nowhere near their level. That said, I was never taken under anybody's wing. I never had a "drag mother," but I still felt like I was beginning to find people I could safely share this side of myself with.

Oddly though, the situation in which I felt most at home was not the weekly drag nights. It was the monthly fetish party. This was the night when the club opened up to any and all who wanted to let their freak flag fly. The only requirement to get in (besides the cover charge) was that you couldn't show up in street clothes. If you tried to get in on fetish night in jeans and a t-shirt you'd be turned away at the door. This night, more than any other at the club, was a night of complete and total acceptance.

While I don't consider myself particularly fetishistic in my dressing choices, I do feel a pull towards the fetish community. I attribute this to how nonjudgmental it all is. When I would get dressed up and work the drag nights I would still be nervous, wondering if I looked feminine enough or if the patrons were thinking to themselves, "She needs to give it up, that just isn't working for her." It may not have been a justified fear, but it was still there. That fear played no part in fetish nights though. The whole vibe of fetish nights was "be whatever you are, nobody will judge you for it." It was freeing in a way that really blew my mind in those early days. I rarely felt more at ease with my feminine self than I did when I strapped on my knee-high boots, black vinyl dress (yes, the same one I wore to *Rocky Horror*), added a collar, and wandered through the fetish crowd gathering up empty glasses. It felt like home. A rather kinky home, I grant, but a home nonetheless.

Since leaving Boston my time at fetish events has been significantly reduced, and while I do miss it, I think it was something that I especially needed at the time. I needed that unqualified acceptance to help me find the confidence to just go out and find myself. As I got a better understanding of what dressing meant to me I didn't need the reassurance of the fetish environment anymore. I still go to such events if they pop up, and adore them deeply, but in hindsight it was largely a stepping stone to discovering and loving this side of myself.

EXPERIMENTING WITH DRESS STYLES

One of the longer processes for me in finding my identity as Vera was to try and settle on some sense of style. This was complicated by a number of things. The first was strictly a financial issue. I just didn't have the money to spend on experimenting with different styles of dress. I very quickly came to appreciate why women shopping for clothes is so much more complicated than guys shopping for clothes.

A man shopping for clothes could not be more basic. For most of us, shirts are either casual (t-shirts) or for work (button down) and pants fit the same basic category (jeans or shorts for casual, slacks for work). Men can mix and match. They can buy a shirt that goes with three different pairs of pants they already have and suddenly one garment purchase gives them three complete outfits. Shoes are also basic. Most guys have a pair or two of sneakers, maybe two pairs of shoes for work (brown and black in my case) and boots. Anything else is superfluous or just for fun.

Shopping for women's clothes is far more complicated. I quickly learned that even though I see a top I like, I may not have any skirts that go with it. So I need a new skirt as well. Now I've got a top and skirt but the color scheme and style doesn't go with any shoes I currently have. Then even after that I may realize that the low neckline is going to look better if set off with a necklace, but I don't have one in the style of this outfit. And on and on and on. And that's not even getting into the sizing issues, which I'll talk about later on. So in short, shopping for women's clothes gets very expensive very quickly if you're trying to put together a complete look.

The other thing that threw me off at first was the fact that most of the dressers and performing queens at Machine were rocking styles that just weren't appropriate for me. To put it simply, I was basically the resident white girl at a club where the other dressers were black or Latina, and the urban clubwear they tended to favor just looked wrong on me. (That's not to say I didn't try to make it work; sometimes you have to fail at something in order to realize it's a bad idea.) The other prominent style that I was exposed to I categorize as "pageant style": big ball gowns and sparkling tiaras. This was something you'd see on the performers more than the girls just coming into the club, but it suited me even less than the clubwear did. I didn't want to feel like I was putting on a costume. I wanted to find a style that just felt like it expressed *me*. But none of what I saw felt quite right, so what's a girl to do?

I honestly floundered a little at first, not really sure how to present myself. Then, after working the monthly fetish night and donning the borrowed vinyl dress that I'd first gotten to wear to *The Rocky Horror Picture Show*, I decided to embrace my whiteness. I decided to go with something that wasn't trying to compete with or measure up to the other girls who frequented the club: I opted instead for goth/punk. As a semi-frequenter of Hot Topic since college, it actually surprises me now that I didn't go for this look sooner. That's probably due to trepidation at the fact that it wasn't what the other girls at the club were dressing in, which just goes to show the importance of finding what works for you rather than trying to gauge off of what everybody else is doing.

Working with the fact that I tend to be pale already.

Goth/punk proved to be a much easier style to take on and it helped solve some of the early shopping issues for me. Since everything is so dark and heavy on the black it allows for much more of the mixing and matching I was used to from wearing men's clothes. I didn't have to have a specific blouse to match a specific skirt because it was all just black. It also simplified my makeup at a time when I needed something that wasn't overly complicated. That's not to say that goth makeup isn't involved, but it removes the intimidating color matching and complimenting the more experienced girls implemented. Dark shades of lipstick and blush coupled with black eyeliner and shadow made my life much easier at a time when that was what I needed. It allowed me to go out with confidence and to work on perfecting the more nuanced makeup I applied later down the line.

Goth/punk never became the only look I had, but it was my go-to for a few years. Knowing that I had this style to fall back on actually gave me a much greater degree of comfort in trying out other things. It no longer felt like some sort of panicked scramble for a look. Before, there was this feeling of "oh my god, I have to find a style quick!" Now it was a much more casual sense of "all right, that works for me so now I can find out what else works." Over the years my goth/punk items have drifted to the back of the closet; they're mainly used now only in performance pieces or if I'm going to more fetish-type events. I've grown and matured away from that look, but at the time I needed it desperately and it served me well.

When advising others on styles, my first piece of advice is to try cuing off of the kinds of looks that you think look good on other women (be they females by birth or other dressers). I'd advise starting with everyday looks as opposed to high glamor, if only to go gentler on your wallet at the start of things. That said, if you feel a pull towards something specific like ball gowns or frilly dresses and not nearly the same pull to a more casual blouse and skirt combination, then don't feel like you have to hold off on what appeals to you most. Follow your instincts and desires first and foremost and then figure out how to make that work for you, rather than trying to find something that works and learning to love it later.

CHAPTER FOUR

PUTTING ON A SHOW

My time working at Machine in Boston was important to finding how all of this was going to fit into my life going forward. As I mentioned before, it gave me my first taste of a real-life community that was accepting and supportive of what I was doing. It also got me up close and personal with drag performers. It didn't take long for me to realize that this was going to be the ideal outlet for me. If I'm being honest, dressing alone at home never really felt like enough. Webcam was ok for a quick thrill but it was just a touch too artificial, too distant and second-hand. But showing off in front of a whooping crowd? This was more my speed.

Let me say flat out that performance is not for everybody. Many people find the very notion to be nerve wracking and highly stressful. For me, though, it was a completely natural progression. I was a performer long before I had any sense of myself as a cross dresser. From a young age I wanted to act. I was a fixture in plays throughout high school and college, and as I mentioned before I even tried (unsuccessfully) to pursue acting professionally. So for me, getting on a stage in front of a crowd was nothing to be afraid of. It felt natural and even energizing. The idea of being able to do that in dress actually gave me the confidence boost I needed at the time. I knew I was still figuring out my style and makeup, but I knew that I could perform.

Performance also helped pull me away from the online world and webcamming. In some ways being on a webcam is similar to performing live. You're still showing off for the entertainment of others. However, I personally adore that live feedback one gets from a real audience. The cheers, the whistles, and the applause are all rather addictive to me. Just seeing people type "nice bod" in chat window doesn't quite measure up. The other thing is that even if you're in a chat room with 50 or more people watching your cam there will always be guys (I hate to stereotype, but it's *always* guys) who will try to demand your undivided attention and think they can order you around. For some of us it's almost a relief to have someone take control like that, but for others it's one of the most frustrating parts of the webcam experience. On webcam I'm derided as a tease if I don't perform some sexual act that a few vocal guys are demanding. In a live show at a club or theater the audience *loves* that I tease them, show just enough skin and move in just the right way to make them want more before I blow a kiss and head offstage. The presence of other physical human beings keeps those who might have been bullies online from pulling the same crap at a stage show. In stage performance you have a certain degree of control over your audience simply because you can choose your venue. This is control you rarely have online, where there will always be at least one guy typing out "SHOW UR COCK!" or sending you pictures of his. Of course, with webcams you can counteract this by developing specific people you cam with rather than getting into group chat situations. But again, for me that never did the trick because I like a mass audience. I do recognize what's true for me but may not be true for others when it comes to this.

Even as a semi-seasoned performer, I have to admit that my first time performing in dress was terrifying. I think that had more to do with my fear of audience expectations rather than general performance nerves. The drag queens who performed at Machine fell largely into two camps: high glam and exquisite dancers. The hostess at the time, Mizery, was a raunchy but highly glamorous performer. Big hair, glittery outfits, and diva attitude ruled the day and she owned that performance space like few others I've seen since. Some of the regulars had a similar vibe while others, usually the physically smaller and lither ones, opted for skimpy outfits and impressive dance moves. These were the ones with more exposed skin who would do high kicks and flashy moves that one would never think possible in high heels. All of this intimidated me because I knew I wasn't either of these things. I wasn't that skilled of a dancer nor was I a high glam pageant-style queen. I was still figuring out my style as a dresser and a performer, but I knew I didn't fall into those categories.

While I consider myself to be a decent dancer (for somebody lacking formal training) I was not of the same caliber as the dancing queens, and I never would be. I knew if I truly dedicated myself to it I would eventually be able to do the glam lip sync approach used by some of the pageant-style performers, but it just wasn't me. So trying to find something in-between was my challenge. I'm not sure I pulled it off those first few times. I performed at a number of the monthly amateur nights, which were actually competitions in addition to being open forums for newcomers. Audience applause would determine the night's winner. I never did win, which didn't surprise me since I was still finding my footing, but I still got a positive reaction. And with each performance I gained a little bit more confidence.

I was also lucky enough that one of the people who saw me perform, Crystal, was herself a regular performer at Jacques Cabaret. Jacques is the only dedicated drag bar in Boston, and actually the only one I've found in the northeast quadrant of the country. Mostly dressers have to settle for drag- or trans-themed nights once a week or less at the local gay bar. There's certainly nothing wrong with that. But a bar that is all about cross dressers and transfolk every single night of the week is a rarity that I was happy to find.

I had actually tried to get bartending work at Jacques before I was hired at Machine. They didn't have an opening for a bartender at the time and I wasn't ready to take a shot at being a performer yet. So to return to Jacques and get to hit the stage there was wonderfully empowering. The amateur nights at Machine might have been my start, but the performances I gave at Jacques made me feel like a true performer and not some boy in a dress just playing at it. I wasn't in competition with other girls; I was just there on the stage for the enjoyment of the patrons. Whether the crowd was large or small, it was always enthusiastic and appreciative and that's the thing I needed most. The foundations I built in Boston gave me the strength to keep pursuing performance no matter where I ended up and I continue to perform to this day at almost every opportunity.

THE POWER OF FRIENDS

I've talked a fair amount about my ex-wife Laura, though in the stories so far we weren't married yet. Before being my wife she was my best friend, and despite our split she still is.

For many years she was my rock and the support at home that I needed, and I hope every dresser is able to find such support, even if some things can't last forever. However, what she could not do, especially in those early days, was be at my side when I went out. With rare exception I was working weeknights at the bar and she was working a normal day job. It simply wasn't reasonable for me to expect her to put in a full day's work and then come out and be with me until midnight or later on the occasions I was performing. *I could barely function with the hours I was keeping, and my day work was only sporadic temping jobs.*

I was fortunate enough, however, to make friends at the night scene, and I had a few from my day job who were willing to come out at those late times and watch me perform. I was lucky enough to have a friend named Christine who was able to attend that first performance I gave as an amateur, and her enthusiasm for what I did went a long way towards keeping me going. She also tended to attend the fetish nights that I talked about earlier. She called me her favorite dance partner, and was another reason that those nights helped me find the confidence in my dressing to reach the comfort level that I now enjoy.

I think it's vital for those of us going out in public to start out doing so at trans- and drag-friendly events, but that alone isn't always enough. As much as I never felt rejected by the regulars at Machine, I knew that I also wasn't truly a part of their world. There was an odd sort of backstage politics at play between certain drag "houses" (which is a whole section of drag performance and life that I was never really a part of). And, to be honest, I also felt like the token white girl. I knew I was welcome to be there, but I didn't really feel totally at ease unless Christine was around.

It was the same when I started performing at Jacques, though with a different friend in attendance. I met Teresa while temping at a cookie factory. We both were temps assigned to sort through a year's worth of invoices, which was laborious and not very engaging. Naturally, as we sorted, we also talked. While I don't advocate coming out about being a dresser to anybody just out of blue, you'll start to get a good sense of who will be ok with that fact not long after getting to know them. So before the end of that day I told her that I performed in drag and where I'd be next. She came with her then-girlfriend to see me perform. So even for that first show in a new venue in front of a new crowd I had people to support me.

Having one or two special friends to accompany you when you go out in dress is something that I think every dresser needs. Sadly, not all of us have it. Depending on how deep in the closet we are or the area we live in, going out may not even be an option (accompanied or not). But if you ever do go out, I highly encourage you to do so with a friend. Going out on your own can lead to second guessing yourself and giving into your insecurities. Having that friend at your side who isn't judging you and is just there to have fun with you is the single best remedy I've found for quelling these fears. The friend could be another dresser, a sibling, a significant other, or even a coworker if you have one that you trust enough. Wherever you find them, that one friend is going to be your best armor against your own fears and doubts about what you're doing.

CLUB GIRL

If there's one aspect of trans culture (male to female trans culture, at least) that I never was able to fully embraced, it was the club scene. Given that I basically started in a bar it's kind of odd that I never felt at home in these settings. Even now it's not my scene. I certainly tried, and there were times I even enjoyed those nights out. But it never felt quite right to me, so I have to admit that my firsthand experience in the trans or drag club scenes that exist in most large cities is pretty limited, and possibly quite dated by now. When people ask me for advice on finding clubs to go to, I have to 'fess up to being a bad resource for this.

I personally found that unless a location is holding a trans-centric event (a "ladies night," if you will) the environment in gay bars and clubs isn't always welcoming to dressers. While dressers can be lumped together with either the "T" or the "Q" in the LGBTQ+ community, that doesn't mean that the rest of those letters know how to react to us. On the occasions I found myself in a gay bar for anything other than a trans night I always felt like I was being looked at by other patrons as a nuisance, somebody who wasn't welcome on a "normal" night. Maybe in my case it was compounded by the fact that I'm generally not attracted to men. It's hard to say definitively.

Even at trans events, whether they were at gay bars or more all-purpose clubs, I found out quickly that there will always be men there who are after sex. And more than that, they will assume that they can fulfill their needs with a cash exchange. This is more an issue in large cities (NYC was worse than Boston in my experience), but I've stopped counting the number of times I've been propositioned in a bar or a club by men who thought my time and my body were for sale. In a way, it's oddly flattering the first couple of times. But it quickly becomes annoying and even degrading. This is not to belittle any dressers or trans persons who do engage in sex work. As far as I'm concerned they have every right to it. However, the number of men who are happy to assume that *any* female-presenting person they encounter in a club is willing to prostitute themselves is disquieting.

To be fair, I've been to some events where I really couldn't blame these men for their assumptions, as much as they may annoy me. In New York City, especially, the honest truth is that many of the trans events at clubs are organized by and built around the presence of sex workers. So in those cases perhaps it was my mistake for being there in the first place when I wasn't looking for that kind of attention. But that doesn't excuse the guys who just won't take a "no" the first time. Nobody ever got forceful with me, thank goodness, but the persistence of these men stops being flattering and starts becoming creepy quite quickly.

I should stress that not all trans events I went to were like that. The ones that were designed more as mixers for the trans community were much less sexually-minded. Of course, that still put me in a bit of a conundrum. Because honestly, one of the things I love to do when I go out in dress is to dance. But the dance clubs always had the oversexed guys trying to buy me, while the friendlier and safer environments rarely had much in the way of dancing. They were more social gatherings and I'm not quite at home in "let's all chat and get to know each other" situations. I socialize fairly well but it takes pressure off for me if the reason for the gathering is something else and socializing is a side activity rather than the focus. If I'm being honest, even at the more subdued mixers there were always men who tended to hang back and just watch. They rarely approached, and they certainly weren't as aggressive as the men in dance clubs, but they were always there. They ogled, they fantasized, and they stared.

I suppose in hindsight what I really needed was a small group of friends to go out with. If I had people who I came with it was so much easier to ignore the elements of a club or a bar that I didn't like and just focus on the fun. "Strength in numbers" probably would have given me the courage to go to an ordinary bar or club and not worry about whether or not it was having a trans night. I never built enough of those kind of relationships with other dressers while I was in New York. I had a few friends like that in Boston, but I wasn't there long enough to really take advantage of them in that way. It was another case where I didn't realize when I was well off. Since leaving New York it's the exception for me to go out to events that I'm not performing at. I just never found an approach to these situations that seemed to work for me consistently.

FINDING BURLESQUE

If there's one thing that I learned quickly upon my move from Boston to New York it's that the world of drag performers was not for me. I found it to be not overly inviting and, to be blunt about it, the scene is just kind of bitchy. I accept that things have likely improved since I first looked into drag, but I can only speak to my experience. Keep in mind I had kind of back-doored my way into drag performance in Boston, and most of the people I was performing alongside warmed to me even before I hit the stage. I had it easy there, though I didn't realize it. Once I got to New York it became much clearer how harsh the drag scene usually is.

To call the drag queen community "cliquey" would be an extreme understatement. First, there's a frightening divide between the pageant queens and everybody else. Drag queens who perform in pageants tend to view themselves as different, and usually better, than other performing queens and that's often made all the worse when they encounter non-performing dressers. Then even within the non-pageant community there's an unsettling amount of politics going on. In larger cities many queens belong to certain "houses" depending on who their "drag mother" was. (This is a term for a mentoring queen who takes a newcomer under her wing.) Now, I have to admit I don't totally get how all of this works because I was never a part of it. I never had a drag mother, and while I've offered advice and help to many dressers over the years I've never really been a drag mother to anybody else either. I'm just not a part of this system. Most of the queens I encountered in New York were quick to pick up on that and turn up their noses at me in a passive aggressive fashion. Imagine every popular high school mean girl cliché ramped up to the max and you have a good idea of what it's like backstage at a typical drag show.

Exacerbating the issue was the fact that I was new to New York. While I wasn't exactly a big deal in Boston, I could be considered a professional performer by the time I left. I was getting paid and was even requested to perform on a few occasions. But in New York nobody cares who you were elsewhere. They only care what you've done in New York City (or if you've been on TV). And if you haven't done anything in the city before, they won't give you the chance to do anything now. So there's a vicious cycle of not getting gigs because you don't have experience in the city, but you can't get experience because you can't get the gigs. This Catch-22 isn't limited to drag, for the record. I tried my hand at stand-up comedy as well while I was in New York and ran into almost the exact same issue. The systems that were in place when I was there were designed to either obstruct the newcomers or to viciously exploit them for the benefit of the established performers. Often it was both.

Don't get me wrong, I wasn't completely shut out. I did do a few drag shows in New York. I even met a few queens that I'm still friends with (obviously they are the exceptions to much of what I'm talking about here). However, by and large the few early gigs I got didn't lead to much else because I didn't have any inside resources the way I did in Boston. I eventually found myself forgoing the stage and turned mostly to modeling as an alternative. And while I enjoyed the modeling, it was largely limited to what I could find through online sites, which was a mixed bag at best, even back then (and appears to have gotten worse in the intervening years).

Then, completely by chance, I was invited to an event by a dresser I knew through social media. She'd just finished a burlesque performance class and the "final" was that all the students got to perform in a little revue. I went as a show of support, but what I saw changed everything about my performing life. The class and the show were put on by Dottie Lux, a wonderful performer who has since moved to the west coast. She and her students opened up a whole new world for me. The students themselves were, of course, a mixed bag in terms of the quality of their performances but there were unifying themes in everything I saw. It wasn't so much about perfectly executed choreography or over-the-top costumes. It was about the *feel* of what was being done. It was communicating a character or story or mood through the dance and the strip tease. And what I felt while watching it rang true and was actually much more in line with what I'd been trying to do in drag shows.

One of the things that had always driven me nuts in drag shows was trying to find a way to keep it interesting. In my opinion you can only watch a queen preen about and lip sync for so long before it starts to all feel the same, no matter how beautiful or energetic they are. I didn't have the raw dancing skill to do the kind moves that would keep that kind of routine fun for three to five minutes. So the way I'd tried to keep it moving was through on-stage costume changes, removing a top layer of clothing to reveal something else underneath. I don't want it to sound like no other drag queens ever did this, but because I couldn't pull together the glamor level of most other queens, my act didn't really gel at those shows. In burlesque, the removing of clothes is not only expected, it's half the point. What you reveal underneath doesn't have to be pristine and sparkly, it can be just about anything (or nothing, as some audiences would prefer). It just has to continue the story and tell the audience something new.

Backstage selfie from a recent Burlesque show.

I'm sure some are asking what differentiates burlesque from stripping. There's two main things. The first is money. People get into stripping to make a living. You *can't* get into burlesque for the money. With the exception of a very small number of workaholic performers, most of us are lucky to break even. If you get paid at all, the odds are it will barely cover your costume and travel expenses. So by and large the people who do it are in it because they love it. Nobody falls into burlesque as a last ditch attempt to pay the bills.

The second thing is that when a stripper performs the whole point is to get naked and show it off. In burlesque, the stripping isn't really the point. Rather, it's the medium. Just to prove this point many burlesque performers aren't at their most naked (usually panties and pasties) until the last ten seconds or so of a three to five minute performance. Good luck trying to be naked for that small a percentage of your stage time at a strip club. A good burlesque performance isn't just about taking off clothes, it's about telling a story in the way that you do it, through what clothes are removed and what is revealed underneath them. These stories can be sexy, or sad, or even scary and disturbing. You're allowed a great deal of freedom in the kind of story you want to tell or character you want to portray so long as clothing removal is part of how you convey it.

Burlesque felt closer to theater to me than drag ever did (which often felt more like elaborate karaoke), and it's probably the most open and inclusive artistic scene I've ever encountered in my life. First of all, it welcomes all body types. Most of the best burlesque performers I've known and seen would be booed off the stage in a strip club because their bodies don't conform to the current standard of beauty. But they're amazing because they tell amazing stories with their bodies and do it to perfection with their choreography. And the choreography does not have to be about flashy moves or splits or any of the other stuff that's often expected in a drag show. It's all about relaying the story of who the performer is being or who they are becoming as they take off more and more of their clothes.

Burlesque is also incredibly welcoming to outsiders. There were almost no opportunities for amateur performers in drag shows, unless your drag mother was somebody with pull. In burlesque the number of shows that are either centered around or are at least open to new performers is huge. Once I decided to start pursuing burlesque I had no trouble at all getting performance slots. They weren't just in hole-in-the-wall bars, either. While drag is very embedded in what is "proper" and established, burlesque thrives on new blood and new ideas. This meant that my first amateur shows were in front of good-sized crowds rather than six people in a bar. The very first one I did was even hosted by noted drag king Murray Hill, who is something of a New York legend. It would have been like Ru Paul hosting an amateur drag show (not a pageant, just a run of the mill show at a small bar with a stage).

The fact that as of this writing I've never been booed, questioned, or looked down on despite the reality that there aren't a great number of trans or genderfluid type performers in burlesque just goes to show how accepting these people are. If the drag community is made up of the bitchy popular kids, then burlesque is the community formed by the outcasts and the weirdos. They don't judge you because they don't want you to judge them. As long as you don't half-ass it on stage and are professional backstage, you can come from anywhere and do nearly anything and you won't be rejected for it. I've found this to be the case everywhere I've been involved in burlesque; this open and welcoming environment is not limited to just the New York scene. That kind of community was a blessing to find and one that I continue to embrace at every opportunity. Are there some divas or sleazy producers on the scene? Sure, just as there are in any artistic medium. But they don't dominate burlesque the way I've seen in drag and other performance scenes.

LIFE WITH THE KINGS

When I talked about finding burlesque I brought up some of the issues that I've had with the drag community (i.e. the egos paired with some pretty elaborate backstage politics), but that was really just with the drag *queen* community. Drag kings, on the other hand, I've never gotten anything but love from. If you don't know what drag kings are, it's the logical inverse of a drag queen: a woman who will don the attire and adopt the mannerisms of masculinity (often to the point of caricature) for the sake of performance. While I encountered a number of drag kings in my time in NYC, the group I became most familiar with was the Brooklyn-based drag troupe Switch 'N Play.

The fact that SNP was a drag *troupe* should tell you the first major difference between the drag king and the drag queen communities. Queens are solo divas. They command the stage and try to outshine everyone, and that "I'm better than everybody else" persona has a tendency to bleed over to the backstage. Drag kings, however, are most often seen in performing groups; in some areas you actually have to hunt to find a drag king who performs primarily as a solo artist. There's an inherent comradery between kings that I never really felt amongst queens, who largely view each other as competition. Maybe it just has to do with what the stereotypes of "masculinity" are (the "bro" mentality) which lend themselves to bonding rather than conflict.

SNP came on my radar when I was looking for gigs in New York, because once a month they held an "Open Drag Night," where anyone doing any kind of drag performance was welcome on the stage. These events were held at the Outpost Lounge in Brooklyn, outside on the patio when the weather permitted. The environment was welcoming, the crowds were enthusiastic, and even though I was often the only queen in attendance I was never made to feel out of place. I was told later by some of the members of SNP that they had been nervous to have me because of the diva reputation that queens have. Thankfully, I didn't live up to that stereotype, and after a while they actually asked me to join the group as their first ever resident queen. I only got to be an actual member of the group for about a year before I left New York, but it was a wonderful group to work with at every point in the process, from rehearsal to performance. And I came away with some amazing friendships that I still cherish.

BIG CITY QUEEN IN A SMALL TOWN

By the time Laura and I (married by then) moved out of New York, we were both more than ready to get out of a big city. We were reaching the point where the desire to start a family was becoming stronger, and while we had been able to afford to live in New York there was no way we would ever be able to afford to raise a child there. Not that we really wanted to raise a child in the city anyway. Both of us wanted something more laid back and less hectic for our future child as well as our own peace of mind.

I don't regret leaving New York. By the time I left I'd gotten whatever I was going to get out of being there. I'd gotten to perform and model, I'd produced and hosted my own show (called "Drags and Dolls") at two different venues in Manhattan, and I'd gotten to experience the club scene. I'd gone to Broadway shows, and I'd made some good friends. I'd tried my hand at stand-up and even acted in a few movies (which never saw proper releases, but what can you do?). So it really was time to leave before the city began to grind me down, because honestly it does that once you start to settle into a routine and are out of new things to try.

That's not to say there aren't things I miss. I miss the friends I left behind, and I try to keep in touch as best as I can. I miss the subways, which might sound odd. There was just something kind of zen about being able to zone out during my commute to work. Now I drive to work, which means I have to focus and can't read a book or pop open my portable DVD player. And I definitely miss some of the opportunities that the city offered when it came to my life as Vera.

You don't get porches like this in the city. Photo by Syd London.

Laura and I settled in Vermont, in the same general region where I'd grown up. It was a case of coming home for me and it's been one of the best things we could have done. Thankfully, opportunities to indulge life as Vera did not entirely vanish. They just became a bit more spaced out and involved a little more effort. While I was in New York I was going out almost every week, either to perform or to a party or something of that nature. Since returning to Vermont it's become more like once or twice a month, but I've reached a point in my life where that pace works for me. If I ever tried to go back to NYC and do the every week thing I think it'd probably burn me out in three months, tops. These days I rather enjoy the slower build up to shows or mixers. And if I need a fix in between I tend to shoot a video or two for my YouTube channel. That said, having to drive at least 90 minutes to get to the closest dressing-friendly event isn't exactly my ideal. But long commutes to things I'd like to do is just a reality of rural living, whether I'm going out as Vera or taking the family to a museum.

One big downside, however, is I've had to become a bit more protective about being discovered by town residents. Having to become more cautious did take some getting used to. In New York I had to take safety into consideration, but as far as people seeing me in dress it really didn't matter. Odds were good that anyone who saw me would never run into me again. Living in a rural area, that's simply not the case. I can't just step out of my front door in a dress because word of that kind of thing can and will spread quickly. And while I hold absolutely no shame about who I am or what I do, I still recognize the reality of people being able to make my life, or more importantly, the lives of my child and her mother, difficult as a result of my dressing.

DEAR MOM

When Laura and I first moved to Vermont, we took up temporary residence with my mother while we house hunted. So this seems as good a place as any to talk about coming out to the woman who brought me into this world. Two frequent questions I get asked are: "When should I come out?" and "How should I do it?" I was lucky in that the person who absolutely had to know, i.e. my ex-wife, found out on her own and never made a big deal of it. I was spared ever having to really come out to her in any kind of planned "we need to talk" fashion. There were various friends that

I've told over the years, but all of them knew me well enough that they either were able to simply roll with it or weren't that surprised in the first place, so that never really felt like a coming out either. The only person I really feel like I've had a proper coming out to is my mother. So I'm going to talk about that, with the caveat that I'm not saying this is the best way to come out to a family member. This is just how it happened for me.

Telling my mother about Vera happened before the move to Vermont, but was something I put off doing for quite a while. I rationalized a number of reasons for this as the years went by (she was still with her bigot husband, I wasn't planning to transition so it wasn't like she'd *have* to know, etc.) but at the heart of it I know that fear was the main one. Not so much fear of rejection—I knew she'd love me no matter what—but fear of doing anything to change the wonderful relationship we'd always had.

Part of what kept me from telling her in the early days was that I knew there would be a great many questions from her, and I wanted to be in a position to actually answer them. If I had come out to her when I was still figuring all of this out and she'd asked me questions about whether I wanted to live as a woman or if I was gay, I wouldn't have been able to answer them. And I was concerned that would make her worry. That was probably my biggest fear: I didn't want to worry her. My mother is a bit like me. She knows how the world should be but isn't blind to how it really is. The world shouldn't care if a boy wears clothes normally worn by girls, but the reality is that some people get very upset by it. That reality would have been a great cause of worry for my mother if I wasn't in a position to be able to reassure her. And I just wouldn't have been able to do that with any confidence in the early days.

By the time I'd found where dressing was fitting into my life, I started to realize that this was a big enough part of who I am that it didn't seem right to keep it from her. I probably didn't go about it the best way. She was visiting me and my wife at the time. I asked her to sit down and said I had something to tell her. She was slightly relieved when I told her that I was a cross dresser and drag performer. She'd thought I was going to say that my wife and I were having a baby, something she rightly knew we weren't ready for at the time. Then the questions came. Once I made it clear that I wasn't going down to the grocery store in a sun dress she became a bit more relaxed.

However, I know that it took her a bit of time to wrap her head fully around it, more than she'd probably ever admit. I offered to show her pictures of myself in dress after that first conversation, thinking that would help her understand, but she declined. It was probably too much at that point. She found her footing fairly quickly, though, and was soon offering me some of her old dresses or jewelry pieces that she thought would fit me.

Her first time seeing me in dress wouldn't come until several years later, during the brief period when Laura and I lived in her house. That was the first year I performed at VT Pride. I came back from the show still in dress, which included fishnet stockings, a short skirt, a tank top, and platform high-heeled boots. She was in the kitchen when I entered the house. I will never forget her first reaction. She paused, looked me over, and said, "You're really tall." We laughed and everything has been relaxed ever since.

She's even become rather philosophical about it. Recently she told that cosmically I may have been meant to be a girl. Not that she'd wanted me to be one. Since I was very young she's told me *many* times how much she'd focused her energies on having a boy. But over dinner she casually noted that she was the first daughter of the first daughter of the first daughter going pretty far back in the family tree, and perhaps it's a bit of cosmic balance that I have such a pronounced feminine side. You may have guessed that my mother is a bit new age-y, and I don't know how much I believe her assertion about my femininity. But it's a notion that makes me smile and she touched me by sharing it.

I'm very lucky, not only because of how well she, Laura, and my friends have taken it, but also by how few people I truly had to come out to. Many dressers find themselves having to come out to significant others, parents, friends, siblings, and more. I don't think it ever really gets easier, because even after some positive responses you never know how the next person is going to take it. But for me, the gradual reveal of this part of myself has only been a freeing experience. It has removed burdens from my life and my state of mind, and it has yet to add them. Hiding forever is isolating, and opening up is terrifying. But it's only through opening up that we can find a way to be ourselves in our lives and not just in our minds.

Part II: Practical Advice

CHAPTER FIVE

EARLY PERILS OF MAKEUP

Once I committed to exploring my femininity, the one area that I floundered in more than any other was makeup. When I started out, my knowledge of makeup was completely confined to stage makeup for plays in high school and college, much of which was put on with the intention of making me look older than I actually was, often significantly so. All of which meant that, despite a certain amount of experience (at least on paper), I really had no clue how to go about improving my feminine appearance through makeup.

During my web chat days I had the benefit of a webcam, which at the time was not very high resolution (thankfully). This meant that, as long as I shaved really closely before going on camera, I could get away with just applying lipstick, a bit of eye shadow, and not much else. Looking back I can see that even this minor application was clumsy. I knew nothing about color selection for the lipstick and I was applying a single color of eye shadow from my eyelids right up to the eyebrow. I know now that you need different shades that work well together: a darker one for the lid itself, a lighter one from the top of the lid to the brow, and possibly a third for the crease to make it all flow. And that's just for a basic look. That's not even getting into anything fancy like wings or smoky eye. I didn't know *any* of this at the time and was flying blind. But again, I got away with it for a while because the image resolution on the webcams of the day was so forgiving.

The real world, on the other hand, isn't as kind to those who don't know how to properly apply makeup. This is where Laura (my fiancé at that point) came into the picture to help me out. She was able to give me a woman's perspective on makeup, which was immensely helpful for me. She'd grown up with it, whereas I was an outsider looking in. She helped me select some color schemes that worked for me and also knew when to let me figure stuff out on my own.

Foundation was something I definitely need help with. One of the things that threw me off when it came to foundation was that most of the dressers at Machine were drag performers, who tend to do much more over-the-top and stylized makeup. I would see them before shows doing layers of white, then dark highlights to create cheekbones, and then skin tone over all of that to create a feminine but also exaggerated look. Frankly, it was daunting, but more than that it created a look that wasn't really what I was going for. As a rule most drag queens aren't really trying to pass as women, and many have an almost caricature approach to their makeup. It's a look that reads well from a distance and under harsh performance lighting, but I wanted to work on something that was more in line with what a "typical" woman would do with makeup.

I actually avoided foundation for a while, partly because I hadn't needed it on webcam and partly became it intimidated me in general. I experimented with just using a concealer to avoid any beard shadow, and while it helped a little it didn't totally do the job. My ex-wife helped set me straight on the fact that since I was a man with facial hair I was going to have to deal in foundation, even when I was clean shaven.

Actual foundation application turned out to be fairly simple. What was trickier was how to get the right shade (and realizing I needed a different shade for summer when I had a tan). There are general guidelines, video tutorials, and even apps that claim to help you find your perfect foundation shade. I find those can point you in the general direction but you're going to have to prepare for a certain amount of trial and error on your first few purchases. Or, if you've got the courage, you can always ask for help from something like the makeup counter at a department store. Trust me, they've heard it before.

I quickly found I had to apply a second layer of foundation in the area around my mouth to ensure no beard shadow bled through. That extra layer evened out with the application of a non-translucent powder. At the time this seemed counter intuitive, because makeup was trending to lighter formulas such as mineral powders rather than heavy makeup. But for dressers that just isn't an option. We have things we have to actively conceal or even create from scratch, so giving our faces a light brush-up just doesn't cut it. We're not just glossing over a few blemishes, we're often building a look from the ground up. I caught onto the basics fairly quickly once my fiancé gave me some hands-on help: a layer of foundation, powder to reduce shine, blush on the cheeks, eye shadow, liner, and of course lipstick. Though I fought them for a while, there would eventually also be false lashes.

I eventually got it down pretty smoothly for a standard makeup job. I'm by no means an expert, which is why I've never done step-by-step makeup tutorials, rather just a few basic rules of thumb. I know what more or less works for me,

but I don't know makeup well enough in the broad strokes
to be a resource beyond that.

THE MAGIC OF LIPSTICK

I don't think there's any single item of makeup that is
enough to make me feel feminine on its own. But if there's
one item that you absolutely can't ignore (and it's the one
I've seen even the most casual dressers gravitate toward) it's
lipstick. I'm not sure what it is about lipstick. Perhaps it's
the fact that it's one of the most immediately noticeable
things you can put on and also one of the easiest to apply.
More than that, it's also the easiest to remove and reapply if
you do it wrong or need to take it off in a hurry.

Of course, I made the same mistake that most dressers make
with their first lipstick purchase: I bought what I can only
describe as "hooker red." You know what I'm talking about:
that overly bright shade of red that can be seen from across
a football field. Honestly, this is an incredibly difficult shade
to pull off, nearly impossible, in fact. And that goes for
cisgender women as well. It's so over the top that it's either
going to stand out as being out of place or you have to overdo
the rest of your look so much to match it that the whole look
becomes almost clown-like. And if that's not enough, it has
a great knack for bringing out any dark coloring that might
be on your upper lip (i.e. any hint of residual stubble is going
to show up all the more when wearing this kind of shade).

Lips are a wonderful thing to emphasize, but they don't need
to be lit up like a neon sign. I've tended to favor darker colors

myself: blood reds or something with a hint of purple. As I've developed Vera further I've even gotten into metallic dark greens from time to time. I suppose that's a bit of a holdover from my goth/punk years, but it's a look I've always preferred for my lips. That's not to say that I never break out the pink shades, but that's only to coordinate with an outfit that is predominantly pink (of which I have precisely three and one of those is a set of pajamas).

Lipstick application is probably the easiest bit of makeup to learn, thanks partly to the aforementioned ease of removing it so you can just keep trying it over and over. That said, you'll want to be able to get it on the first go before you start going out in public: removed lipstick does leave some traces, especially if it gets smudged beyond the boundaries of the lips themselves. In the early days there's certainly nothing wrong with practicing repeatedly in front of the mirror until you feel comfortable applying it.

I'm lucky because I'm rather fond of the shape of my mouth. I know there are dressers out there who bemoan their thin lips. And while I understand this, I would urge them to resist the temptation to try and paint beyond the confines of their natural lips to make them look bigger. Sometimes you can get away with it from a distance, or even in a carefully lit photograph. But up close it's going to show, even if you know what you're doing. And it's going to look overly made up at best or comical at worst.

Making sure it's just right.

In terms of thickening lips, there are "lip plumpers" out there which claim to plump up your lips after application. I've only ever tried one of these, but I saw absolutely no difference, not even when I took before and after pictures and scrutinized them side by side. That's not to say that none of them work, but from what I can find even the "good" ones have short-lived effects. And the idea of something causing a swelling reaction on my body is personally something that kind of freaks me out a little bit. There are other devices that claim to plump lips through various means (usually some form of suction) but again, from what I can find, they either don't work as claimed, have very short-lived results, or appear to be potentially hazardous. I strongly stress that it's best to just work with what you have, even if it's not your ideal.

I'm not a huge fan of lip lining either. This is something I mostly see older dressers trying, as it's a bit of a dated technique. But even if it's a look you like, unless you truly know what you're doing it just doesn't look natural. I'll grant that moist-looking deep shades of red don't look natural either, but that's more of an exaggeration of what is naturally there. Lip lining on top of that (or underneath it, if you're going to get technical) is just a step too far more often than not. I've seen stage performers pull it off, but I advise against it for just walking around. I kind of feel the same about most glosses. I like glossy shades of lipstick, but often when I see a separate gloss applied over lipstick the effect is over the top. Since it's not always tinted, or at least not as clearly as lipstick itself, people tend to overdo it. To me, the result of this tends to look like somebody has syrup on their lips and needs to wipe their mouth more than anything else. It can work but, again, moderation is the idea here. Gloss applied conservatively can give lips a nice pop.

One of the other options is something that's tempting but has its drawbacks: lip stains. There are two advantages. The first is ease of application. Many have a pen-like applicator which is easier for beginners to use than a traditional tube of lipstick and is less likely to go beyond where you want it to because you can see the point of contact more clearly. The second is that it doesn't require reapplication throughout the day. Lipstick (especially a glossier shade) rubs off notoriously easily, which means it gets on your food, the rims of glasses, and all over anybody you're getting intimate with. Even if you're not planning to eat anything or kiss anybody, most normal shades of lipstick will start to fade after a few hours. Lip stain takes those issues out of the equation. However, they last so long that if you have to go about your day in boy mode, even the next morning, you may find yourself viciously trying to rub the lip stain off your lips. It can be done but isn't exactly a pleasant experience. So keep in mind when the next time you need to look like a boy is going to be. If it's not for a while then stain away. Otherwise, proceed with discretion with these products.

IT'S ALL IN THE EYES

When it comes to makeup there's one part of the face that has more individual components than any other: the eyes. There's so much to take into consideration: eyebrow shape, eye liner, eye shadow, and eye lashes all come into play. Each of these aspects requires careful coordination with the others to create a complete look, so we'll start at the literal top.

Eyebrow shape is a bit of a tricky issue. As dressers, most of us don't want to have thick bushy eyebrows. At the same time there's only so much we can actually do to the brow itself in terms of giving it a more feminine shape. You can pluck or wax some of the errant hairs to eliminate any unibrow and give a bit of shape. Unfortunately, if you go all out and truly style the eyebrow it's going to look strange when you're out and about in male mode. Speaking for myself, I've taken a bit of a minimalistic, two-fold approach. First I pluck the stray hairs, mostly the ones that fall between my two brows. I don't really have a unibrow but there are some hairs that turn up in that middle space if I don't get them. Other than that I use makeup to fake a thinner brow than I actually have. When I apply my foundation I put the concealing powder over my eyebrow and then pencil in a thinner brow with a brown eye lining pencil. I don't put it higher than the brown is normally or create some kind of ridiculous arch, which is a common drag queen technique. Instead, I follow the actual arch of my brow, only filling in a strip in the middle rather than the whole brow. Basically I'm highlighting the brow shape I wish I had. This creates an illusion that works well, even fairly close up.

Next up is lining the eyes. This is one of those areas that's going take a bit of practice. It took years for me to get good at it. Personally, I just have a very difficult time staying still and not blinking when a pencil is brought so close to my eyeball. I've found it easier with the eyeliners that twist out of a tube, a bit like lipstick, rather than the actual pencils. The main thing with eyeliner is to not overdo it. It's very easy to end up looking like a raccoon, especially if you opt for a black liner. You're going to want a thin line along the bottom lid as close to the lash line as you can get it. I personally don't line my upper lid because I wear false lashes (which we'll get to) and those cover any upper lining

I'd do anyway. However, if you're using mascara or not doing anything with lashes then you'll want a similarly thin line on the upper lid as well.

While I mentioned both the pencil and lipstick-style eyeliners there are also the increasingly popular liquid liners. I've opted to steer clear of these for the most part because I find them to be far less forgiving if you accidently slip. Applied correctly the effect can be striking, especially on the upper lid. But as mentioned, I don't line my upper lid anyway so the appeal of liquid liners is rather lost on me. If it's something you think you want to try it will take practice, as with everything.

Next up is eye shadow. There are a couple of pit falls with eye shadow. The first is the tendency to overdo it. Any dresser who uses drag queens as a point of reference rather than everyday women may find themselves going over the top. Drag queens love eye shadow. As mentioned before, some will even shadow over their eyebrows (often after first applying a layer of glue over the brow so the makeup sticks in a way it otherwise wouldn't due to the hairs) and draw in brows above that just to go a little *more* over the top. There's also a prevalence of sparkles, glitter, and extremely bright colors. And all of this works for drag queens. Most dressers, however, will want a more reserved look. If you're going to a special event or club that's one thing, but for the most part eye shadow should be more on the subtle side.

The other mistake many first timers make is using a single shade of shadow from the lid to the brow. I used to do this with black during my goth phase. This is a bit of a bold look, but it also flattens out your features and you lose contour and dimension. You always want to be dealing with at least two shades of eye shadow, either complimentary shades or darker and lighter shades of the same color. Whichever color is darker goes directly on the upper eyelid while the lighter color fills in from the top of the eyelid to the eyebrow. This transition of color is what causes the shadowing effect that gives the product its name in the first place, and it's not uncommon to have a single line of transitional color between the two shades at the point where the eyelid ends.

A great product for first timers are matched sets of colors that have been selected to go well together, and in some cases even to compliment specific eye colors. As you gain more experience and confidence you can start experimenting with shades on your own but in the early days these little matched sets will save you from the hazards of trial and error. Your eye color should be a factor in your decisions, as should the other makeup you're planning to use such as lipstick. While you don't necessarily want to exactly match eye colors to your lip color, you also don't want to be putting on a shade of purple lipstick and then orange eye shadow. Hopefully the colors you plan to be wearing are also factored in to all of this to some degree. I wish I could offer more concrete coloring rules, but color theory is not exactly my area of expertise.

Now we reach eyelashes. Long dark lashes are considered particularly feminine, and there are a few ways to go about getting them. The first is mascara, which has both advantages and drawbacks. The first drawback is the obvious cliché of poking yourself in the eye with the brush. While you'll get better with practice, it is going to sting the first few times you do it, so be prepared for that. The other issue with mascara is that it tends to either run or be difficult to get off. A classic mascara can run with tears or sweat, and tears are not an uncommon response to sticking things so close to your eyes. However, I still recommend that risk over a waterproof mascara, which is going to be difficult to get off at the end of the night. This might be a benefit to a woman who can wake up, refresh the mascara, and go to work. For those of us whose daily lives are in male mode it becomes something that draws attention in a way that we generally don't want.

The other thing about mascaras is to remember that the commercials lie to you. Actually, it should be understood that makeup commercials in general lie to you, just by the simple fact that they show you women whose makeup was applied by skilled and trained professionals and then act as though you can easily replicate the look at home. But beyond that basic lie, mascara commercials go above and beyond in their deception. As much as any given mascara can claim to be "lengthening," "volumizing," or "enhancing," the simple truth is that your eyelashes are only so long and so thick by their very nature. Even the best mascara will never create the same show-stopping effect that you get from using false lashes (which is why, if you read the fine print of mascara ads, you'll often see that they admit to using at least some false lashes to enhance the image in the ad). You'll still get some results but keep your expectations in check.

This of course transitions things directly into false lashes. Make no mistake: they were created by the devil. Only pure evil could devise something so infuriating to apply yet looks so amazing that you sell yourself short if you don't use it. I swear by false lashes, but I also have no illusions about what a huge pain they are to apply properly. Even after doing it for years this is still the part of getting all done up that I dread the most.

You'll find false lashes falling into three general categories. The first are realistic lashes that are meant to blend in with your own natural lashes and give them a fuller and longer look beyond what would be possible with mascara alone. Using these types of lashes, due to their more subtle appearance, it may still be necessary to apply eyeliner on the upper lid and then mascara to blend them in with your natural lashes. The second category is fuller and a bit flashy, sometimes incorporating small gems or other sparkly accents, and has a slightly exaggerated shape, usually tapering out to be wider on the outer edge of the lash, but the lashes themselves aren't so over the top as to be cartoonish. These are my preferred type of lashes. They work for stage performance as they're fun and playful, but not so much that they can't be worn in an everyday situation. The third type are so over the top that nobody will mistake them for real in a million years. These types of lashes often come in bright colors or integrate feathers or other large accents. They're popular with some performers and at Halloween, and I'll admit to using them more often in my shows of late. However, for day-to-day wear I would not recommend them.

Regardless of the style of lash the application is pretty much the same. Let me start by saying that I personally find it infinitely easier to apply a lash by hand than trying to use the handling tongs that are sometimes included with the lashes.

First, you're going to want to bend the lash a little bit so it takes on the curve of your eyelid. Failing to do this makes it more difficult to line everything up properly. You may even find you need to take some scissors and trim off a little bit if the lashes are wider than your lids. Next comes the application of lash glue, which you want to apply evenly and not in big gobs. Some use toothpicks to apply it to the edge of the lash. I do it directly, but either way works. I will caution that you have to be pretty confident to just applying the glue directly as I do because it only takes one errant squeeze of the glue to end up with too much. Once you have the glue on the lash you'll actually want to wait almost a minute and blow on the glue a little. The idea is to have it start to set slightly, making it less fluid and more tacky. This will help it stay in place when you put it on your eyelid, because the biggest issue is if it slips before the glue sets. If that happens you end up not only with a skewed lash but smeared glue on your eyelid.

Once you've put it in place do your best to just stay still and blink as little as possible while it sets. Once it has set you can go about your makeup routine as usual. I've seen people argue over whether it's better to apply false lashes early or late in the whole process. Doing them at the beginning means you won't risk smudging any makeup you've already applied. However, if you plan to reuse them (which you can do if you removed them carefully enough that they don't tear) you're likely to end up with eye shadow on them if you apply makeup after they're on. At this point lashes are one of the last things I put on because I've been doing it enough that I rarely have to take a second try at it (though it does still happen sometimes). Once they're on you should be set for the night. The glue that comes with false lashes generally holds well even against sweat. Just be careful when you peel them off. Not only so you can reuse them, but you don't want to accidentally pull out any of your natural lashes in the process. Slow and steady is the way to remove. There'll be a little lingering lash glue, but usually I just rub it off as if it's just unusually aggressive eye gunk like you get in the mornings. Apparently magnetic lashes are becoming a thing, but I have yet to try them and I'm inclined to keep my faith in glue.

CHAPTER SIX

LET'S GO SHOPPING

One of the great obstacles for so many dressers is that of actually acquiring clothing. This means shopping. It's something that thrills and terrifies so many of us. We tend to be convinced that if we go into a store and start looking at women's clothing that other customers or the people who work there will assume we're some kind of fetishistic perverts. This fear turns what should be an exciting and enjoyable experience into a source of great fear and stress. That's not to say there's no inherent stress in shopping for women's clothes already, but much of it we manufacture and heap onto ourselves.

The thing that we must all remember is that store employees and fellow customers don't care about us. Unless we behave like we're doing something wrong there is no reason for other customers to take much notice of us at all. As for the store employees, they don't care who you're shopping for. As long as you're spending money it makes no difference to them whether you're shopping for yourself or somebody else.

Which brings up a basic false assumption many dressers make: thanks to fear, we believe that anyone who notices us shopping for women's clothes knows we're buying them for ourselves. In truth, very few people will make that connection. If they give our shopping any thought at all they're going to assume we're shopping for a wife or girlfriend. There is no reason for them to think we're shopping for ourselves unless we somehow indicate that.

And in the case of store employees, even if they suspect that we're buying for ourselves they aren't going to care.

The one exception to the above statements has to do with those of us who reside in small towns. I'll readily grant that going out shopping was much easier when I was living in a large city and knew there was no way any of the people working or shopping in the store knew me personally. So even if I couldn't completely quell the fear of being judged, I could at least reassure myself that judgement would be from people who would never see me again. That isn't necessarily the case in smaller towns. If you live in a more rural area and go to a store to buy women's clothes it's much more likely that you will see someone there who knows you. This is doubly difficult if you are known to be single or there's wide gap between the size you wear and the one your girlfriend or wife wears, because someone who knows these things may put two and two together. With this in mind, those who are closeted and living in smaller towns may want to consider traveling to the closest city to do any in-store shopping.

It's also worth pointing out that it's more likely to raise a few eyebrows if you're buying makeup. When you're buying women's clothes it's easy for others to rationalize that you're buying an outfit for a female acquaintance or significant other. However, men generally don't buy makeup for women, even as a gift. That said, the same basic rule applies: so long as you don't act like it's anything weird then neither will anyone else. The easiest weapon you have to combat awkwardness is your own attitude. If you behave like it's just the most ordinary thing in the world for a man to buy lipstick and eye shadow then everyone else will as well. Even if they think in their heads that it's odd, they won't say anything if you act like it's normal, because then it makes them the ones acting weird about it. Nobody likes to feel like the odd one out. If you set the tone of it being normal the vast majority of people around you will follow suit.

Of course, thanks to the marvel of the Internet, it's not actually necessary to set foot in a store at all if you truly don't want to. Dressers who can't get over their fears of in-store shopping, or just don't have stores that cater to their sense of style, can always turn to online stores to buy outfits. This does come with several inherent disadvantages, however. The first has to do with the simple fact that things don't always look the same in person as they do online. Different lighting may cause the color to appear different. You can't feel the texture of the fabric or be sure of the quality of the stitching. Sizing becomes even more of a crap shoot than it already is. In a store, quickly holding an item against yourself can confirm that it'll fit the way you expect. So always be sure you're familiar with the return policy of any online store you buy from since, in my experience, you're more likely to end up with something that doesn't quite work the way you hoped.

ONE SIZE FITS ALL? YEAH RIGHT

One of the more frequent questions I get is how to determine what your size is in women's clothing. The sad truth is that there is no hard and fast rule for this, because women's sizing is completely arbitrary. When you go to buy a pair of trousers as a man, the sizing is in inches (32x34, for instance, is a 32-inch waist and 34 inches long in the legs) and inches don't change no matter what company made it. But when it comes to women's clothing a size 12 in one brand may not be the same as a size 12 in another brand, which is why I tend to be between 10 and 14. If you take your measurements with a tape measure (the limp tailor's kind, not the ridged contractor's kind) then you'll find some guides online that should give the ballpark of your size. But expect to find that sometimes you come in a size below that and sometimes you come in a size above that.

Sizing in general is going to be a bit of a minefield, and likely will vary depending on the type of garment you're purchasing. By and large men are taller than women, which can cause its own set of issues. The biggest for me has to do with sleeve length. I rarely purchase anything with sleeves, and not just because of a style choice. For the most part, I can squeeze into women's clothing sized 10 to 14, which is a "large" shirt or blouse. However, sleeves throw this completely out of whack. My arms are not muscular but still cause me problems since they are generally bulkier than most women's. Assuming I can even get my arms comfortably into the sleeves in the first place, the odds are good that the sleeves will end short of my wrist. This means that a shirt, blouse, or coat that would otherwise be a decent fit looks comically undersized because of how ill-fitting the sleeves are.

Being tall in general is an issue, and going up in sizes only does so much to help. I stand 6 feet tall before I put on heels, which puts me quite a bit above the "average" woman that most clothes are theoretically made for. Aside from sleeves, this mostly becomes an issue with dresses—shorter dresses if I'm being specific. It's not that big of an issue if a dress designed to go lower than the knee instead ends up being slightly above the knee on me. I may find, however, that something meant to end at the upper thigh on most women, on me ends up covering... not much at all. As a result, if I want a shorter look I largely have to opt for skirts instead of dresses. Otherwise my ass ends up hanging out. This is why I always stress that you know what the return policy is from anywhere that you're buying. Even when it *should* fit, it doesn't always.

There's also the aspect that I talked about before: shopping as a woman is just different than shopping as a man. To reiterate, as a man you can go to a store and just buy a shirt with a fair degree of confidence that you have pants that will match it. Shopping for feminine clothes means you always have to have a complete outfit in mind. You're going to be spending more as a woman in any one shopping trip than you would as a man just to be sure you've acquired a complete outfit and not simply a single item that doesn't match anything your already have. Of course, dresses simplify things (as opposed to matching tops with bottoms), but then you may run into the height issue I just talked about, so how much that actually helps you may vary.

IF YOU CAN'T TUCK IT...

As a man trying to appear as much like a woman as possible, there's one rather noticeable roadblock in the feminine appearance of any male-to-female cross dresser: it hangs between our legs and has a couple of friends. Clothes designed to be worn by women, especially pants, tend to be rather tight in the crotch, leading to a very telltale bulge for dressers. Even a clingy skirt or dress can show the outline of something that betrays our origin as a male. So if we intend to go out in public and not be borderline obscene in our appearance we need to hide it or, more accurately, tuck it away. Now, we don't *have* to do this, but it certainly is more comfortable for most of us to not have such an obvious give-away as a crotch bulge.

It's called tucking because that's exactly what you're doing. You're tucking your goods away between your legs to create a look that is as smooth as possible. It sounds simple enough but there are some complications. The first has to do with needing the right garment to actually keep the tuck in place. Unless you plan to clench your thighs together really tightly and shuffle everywhere, you need underwear that will actually keep things snugly where you put them. In my early days I actually used medical or duct tape to accomplish this, which I don't recommend for what I hope are self-evident reasons. So that means you need a gaff.

A gaff is basically a thong made specifically for cross dressers. They're not difficult to find. In fact, they're a dime a dozen on the Internet (well, more like $25-$40 per pair, but they're worth it). Compared to a normal thong worn by a woman, a gaff is much thicker in the band that goes between your legs, which means it'll actually cover and hold everything there that would otherwise spill out the bottom and sides. Some of you may be wondering if a fuller pair of women's underwear (i.e. granny panties) would do the same trick, but the answer to that is "not really." It's not enough that there's more fabric there to cover everything. The elastic along the edges also has to be strong enough to hold everything in place as well. A gaff is designed for that; underwear made for women is not. Without a gaff you're almost guaranteed to come un-tucked when you least want that to happen.

Now the nice thing about a gaff is that you can either wear it as your underwear or, since they're mostly thong-styled, you can put a fuller pair of panties over it if you wish. If you hunt around you can even find some gaffs with an artificial camel toe at the front to complete the illusion even in something like leggings or yoga pants.

So now you've got a gaff and are ready to tuck everything back. But there's a trick to it, and it has to do with the testicles. You'll quickly find that these are actually a bigger issue to try and hide than your penis. They're more apt to shift around and find a way to slip outside of the gaff. And frankly, it's not enough to just tuck them between your legs because you're liable to squeeze them uncomfortably just by sitting down. The solution is actually fairly simple: put them back where they came from. In the very early days of your life your testicles weren't in your scrotum, they were in little cavities in your lower abdomen. Then down the line they dropped and fell into your scrotum.

Believe it or not, those cavities are still there and you can push your testicles back up into them. There's actually a decent chance you've done it once or twice by accident just by crossing your legs the wrong way. It's not exactly a pleasant sensation but most don't find it to be outright painful, and it's something you can get used to with time and practice. That said, listen to your body. If trying to do this results in legitimate pain, or if the discomfort builds to the point of crossing over into true pain, then you should stop.

Once those are up and away it's much easier to tuck your penis and empty scrotum between your legs and then keep them there by putting on the gaff. Once your empty scrotum is tucked up in the gaff, your testicles will stay in the cavities because the tightness of the gaff should squeeze your scrotum firmly enough that it flattens out the empty space for them to drop back down into.

There's an alternate option to all of this (besides just not bothering, of course) usually called "up-tucking." Rather than tucking your penis between your legs, this involves pressing it up against your abdomen above your genitals (where your pubic hair is) and then wearing something very tight and confined like Spanx or control top pantyhose, or possibly taping it there snuggly. Your testicles can still be returned to their cavity, with pressure from the tight garment or tape applied to the scrotum to keep it pressed against the body which will prevent the testes from dropping back down, just like with a standard tuck. This is a technique that I've seen primarily endorsed by those who, for one reason or another, don't want to use a gaff or sometimes don't want to wear panties at all. (This is where the use of tape rather than a tight undergarment might come into play.) In the case of the latter it should be noted the trying to hold a traditional tuck with tape generally won't work for long because you're liable to sweat the adhesive off the tape. This was part of the reason I stopped taping and started using gaffs.

There are some drawbacks to up-tucking, particularly if you're using tape. Frankly, it is going to hurt when you pull it off, even if you've taken the precaution of closely trimming or shaving your pubic hair. Also, if you've opted for tape that makes it much more of an issue to use the bathroom. With a normal tuck you can go the bathroom as normal and just re-tuck after. If you're incorporating tape in any way you'll have to reapply the tape, and it will be less sticky with each reapplication and may require you to carry extra tape with you. Even if you're up-tucking with Spanx or pantyhose that still leaves another issue. This technique is not going to completely eliminate the bulge. It simply reduces it by pressing your genitals against your lower abdomen. You'll be able to get away with it in loose skirts and dresses, and possibly even jeans so long as you line up the slight bulge of your penis with the zipper. However, tight pants, shorts, leggings, or anything clingy are going to be trickier to pull off with this method.

Another issue with up-tucking is that the bulge becomes more noticeable if you get an erection. One of the benefits of a traditional tuck (which, I'll note here, is really only possible to accomplish while you're in a flaccid state, so if you are aroused by your dressing it may take some mind over matter practice to remain limp so you can complete the process) is that, once you've done it, an erection doesn't make it more noticeable because it's just swelling between your legs. In fact, being tucked back tends to inhibit the degree to which you can physically become aroused at all for as long as you're maintaining the tuck, which may be either a benefit or drawback depending on your own preferences or intended activities. But don't worry, it won't inhibit anything long term.

No tuck is 100% foolproof. Certain movements, or more likely sweat, could cause things to shift and come loose. This is a particular hazard on the dance floor, where you're likely to sweat as well as move in ways that may jostle things free. In some cases you can basically double up the security measures by tucking with a gaff and then having Spanx or pantyhose over that. It's far less likely to come untucked, but is, in my opinion, the least comfortable solution to the problem. If you find this whole process too uncomfortable to do for long periods of time you can still use the gaff as a normal thong, with your testicles and penis pressed against your abdomen by the gaff in the same manner as the up-tuck. There will still be a bulge, but the strong elastic of the gaff will keep things pressed snuggly and minimize the appearance of that bulge. That will be enough for you to get away with more flowing, loose skirts and dresses. Though for tighter pants or leggings you really are going to want to do a full tuck.

HEAD OVER HEELS

Oh the shoes, *the shoes*! Where does one even start with these things? Let's start with the blunt and unpleasant truth: there are far too many of them and they're too expensive. But they're *so* pretty! There really is nothing that sets off an outfit quite like a properly matched pair of shoes. The shoes just by themselves can say so much. A flirty, strappy sandal sends a different message than earthy, woven wedges. Then there's black leather boots which are saying something different from short-heeled sling backs. And that's not even getting into the area of "Come F*ck Me" pumps.

For the most part, dressers will gravitate towards heels. Heels, by their very nature, are simply more feminine than flats, at least according to our society. Aside from a few small touches, a flat woman's shoe doesn't feel all that different from man's loafer, and given that dressing is just as much about feeling feminine as looking it, most of us skip the flats and go straight for the high heels. And with heels there's the added benefit of what they do for your legs and your rear end. They put you into a posture that really elongates the leg and lifts up the butt, both things that men wanting to dress as women are looking for.

There's a kind of magic in finding that perfect pair.

Of course, heels come with their own share of hazards. A twisted ankle is the first thing that comes to mind. But even if you're not completely falling all over yourself, you still risk not looking quite right if you don't take the time to practice walking in heels. As much as many of us want to go big or go home right off the bat, I have to stress the need to start short and work your way up. Many dressers who've finally worked up the courage to buy heels for the first time go over the top and grab the 5-inch stilettos which, as a starting point, is a recipe for instant pain. You don't climb Everest your first time hiking. Work your way up to it.

For a first pair of heels I recommend two things specifically. The first is a reasonable height. You don't want to start too tall. But you also don't want to start too small when it comes to how much surface area the heel has. I recommend a thick, 3-inch heel to start out with. Second is a strap. Now, the strap can be a sling-back, or it can be a strap that goes over the top of the foot. Either way I recommend it because it will secure the shoe to your foot while you're getting the hang of walking in heels. Most dressers feel that pumps are the sexiest and most feminine of heels. I'm not going to debate that either way, but the problem is that if you don't know how to walk in them they tend to pop off the back of your foot. This is a multi-step learning process. First comes learning how to walk and not fall down, and then after you've got that down you can start to explore strapless shoes and work on keeping them on your feet without a strap. Over time you can work your way up to a higher heel with a smaller surface area. If you want to go high but feel nervous in stilettos, wedges are a great compromise.

More than anything, practice makes perfect. And it's not enough to just put on a pair of heels and walk up and down your hallway a few times. I recommend putting on heels and just going about your normal day at home if you can. This will allow you get used to the shoes just being on, and will also give you the opportunity to confront things that dressers don't always think to practice, like going up and down stairs. You'd be amazed how often I see dressers, and even cisgender women, clutching onto railings as they wobble their way up or down a flight of stairs. Don't be that girl.

What I mentioned before about pumps popping off the back of your foot brings up another issue: shoes are really something you should try before you buy. I know that not all of us have the nerve or the freedom to go to the local shoe store and start trying on heels. Plus, most of us have larger and wider feet than most women, so we're stuck with the small selection of size 11 and up in the back of the store. So you may not be able to try the shoes on first and be limited to Internet shopping. But if nothing else, take a good long look at the return policy before you buy something online.

When you buy shoes, even as a man, you can't just find your size and go. You have to put them on, take a few steps, and make sure they feel right. Because sometimes they just don't, even when they're the correct size. This is doubly true with women's shoes. With clothes you can do all right just buying in your size since there's only so far off the rails clothes can go if you're in the ballpark. An ill-fitting shoe, however, will ruin your entire night faster than anything else. That said, figuring out your size is easier than with clothing.

The rule of thumb is to go up a size and half from your male foot size, opting for a wide fit if needed.

Once you're shod and ready to go out you're going to realize quickly that your feet are going to hurt. Whether you're able to walk well in heels or not, they *will* hurt after a while. And the general rule is that the higher the heel, the faster they'll start to hurt. What's more, getting off your feet for a little bit doesn't help like you'd think it would. If you go out dancing in heels and start to feel the pain of it, you'll probably go sit at the bar or somewhere to rest your feet. Unfortunately, when you get off the barstool, you put your feet right back in the situation that they were trying to recover from, and it can be like a jolt of electricity up your legs if you're not prepared for it. This is another area that extended at-home practice comes in handy. You'll want to get a sense of how long you can stand being in the various shoes that you have. Armed with this knowledge you'll be able to select shoes that won't kill you when you're going out for a long night of dancing. So perhaps think about saving those 5-inch stilettos for a few hours out to dinner where you aren't going to be on your feet the whole time.

There are a few cheats out there for people who are having trouble with any of this, be it the balance or the pain. I mentioned wedges already, which are more stable than traditional heels but can still go quite high and give that same lifting affect to the legs and rear end. I talked about the strap in reference to early practice, but if you don't want to get rid of it there's no need to. It will always help ensure that shoe stays on your foot if that's an area of worry for you. There's also platform heels, which is a trick I used back in my more punk/goth days working at the bar. I had a pair of knee-high black boots that were platformed. What this meant was that the heel of the boot was about 6 inches, but because the front part of the shoe was also lifted the actual incline of my foot was the equivalent of a 3-inch heel. I was able to have the high heel without the pain of the steep incline. However, the drawback to this method is that it adds even more to your height than a normal heel does. For the shorter amongst us this might not be an issue. But speaking as someone who is 6 feet tall when standing flat-footed, I tend to feel like my height is my major give away already and I'm not always keen to draw attention to it.

Heels are something you're going to find yourself buying far more of then you probably intend. As mentioned earlier, men tend to have a very small selection of shoes: boots, sneakers, dress shoes, and maybe sandals depending on the local weather. Most men won't have more than two of any of those given types, if that. With women's shoes there are never enough. Matching color and style to the rest of the outfit is such a part of dressing feminine you'll quickly realize there isn't a "standard" shoe you'll keep going back to for every outfit. Some are more versatile than others (black goes with the most things) but you'll find yourself wishing you had something that matched the new dress a little better and suddenly another pair of heels is occupying space in your closet. This is the root my own love/hate relationship with shoes. They look amazing but are a pain on my feet and my wallet. Just one more thing that you have to find balance with (sorry, I'm not above the occasional pun).

ACCESSORIZING

Of course there's much more to an outfit than just the clothes: there's how you accessorize! This primarily takes the form of jewelry, but it can also be belts, gloves, hair clips, or any number of add-ons to enhance or complete a look. When adding little things it's incredibly easy to go overboard, so it's best to always remember the advice of Coco Chanel: "When accessorizing always take off the last thing you put on." This plays to the fact dressers tend to get overexcited and put on at least one thing too many.

In terms of specifics, what you have available to you for accessories is going to be heavily dependent on the style of clothing you're wearing. I have some more classic (almost vintage-looking) outfits that I love to add a flower in the hair for. However, as much as I love my fabric flower, I wouldn't add that if I'm going for a more urban or casual look (t-shirt and jeans, for instance). I also have quite a few accessories left over from my goth days that don't get much use anymore. Things like a pentagram necklace, chain bracelet, and a leather choker now tend to sit at the back of the accessories drawer because they're simply no longer appropriate for most of my outfits.

Accessories really are a fun thing to just experiment with, and it's surprisingly easy to pick up some very inexpensive options that still look nice. Be slightly cautious of over-the-top costume jewelry such as oversized pearls or ludicrously large jeweled rings. These sorts of items are popular with performing drag queens, but that's due to their camp value and the fact that they can be seen from a distance, thereby playing to the back of the audience. These aren't the sorts of things you'll generally want to go out of the house wearing unless it's really your goal to go for a theatrical look that draws attention. Of course, if that's what you're going for, then by all means.

Chokers and thin fabric scarves are popular amongst many dressers because they cover up the Adam's apple. Honestly, I don't feel that this feature is as big a giveaway as many dressers fear, unless it's unusually pronounced. It can be the sort of thing that people look to if they're unsure about somebody's gender but rarely will people just zero in on it. Many of us are insecure about it nonetheless and a choker or a scarf can cover it up and put us more at ease. Ultimately, these sorts of accessories probably have more value for their calming effect on those who need it rather than as an actual accessory. If I'm being honest, chokers and scarves are not appropriate to an exceptionally wide range of styles.

Overall, accessories really don't require much guidance beyond "don't overdo it." There is one specifically, however, which can be a bit tricky for many dressers: earrings. The main issue here is whether or not to pierce your ears. The thing to remember is that if you don't keep something in your piercings most of the time, they close up. And more than that, even if they close they leave a scar, meaning people can tell if you used to have piercings. So if you get your ears pierced mainly for your dressing life you still have to deal with it day to day, one way or the other. Some of us work in offices where a man with earrings would be frowned upon or possibly even forbidden by an office dress code. I'm not in such a situation, but I still opted to not pierce my ears for a very long time. This is because, by and large, I just didn't care for the pierced ear look on myself as a man. I felt that I looked like a pirate. Some time ago I did have one ear pierced, but I never got the other one because I didn't think it would look right. I let that one piercing close up and kept it like that for about a decade. I did eventually get my ears pierced, but that was part of a bigger shift in my life that I'm going to go into more detail in a later chapter. Once I did pierce my ears I had some simple loops and basic studs for day-to-day wear and more fun things like big hoops or sparkling dangly earrings for when I'd go out in dress.

Not piercing your ears doesn't mean you'll have no options for earrings, but it does limit you rather severely. There are certainly clip on earrings available in stores and online but there are a few inherent problems with them that you should know going in. The first is that, after a while, your ears are going to be sore. Even if you get something very light weight, it's still pinching the lobe of your ear to stay in place. Even if it's got nice soft foam pads, a full day with these on and you're going to feel it when you take them off. Next is the issue of quality. You can certainly get some that look nice enough, but clip on earrings are almost invariably made of low quality metals. It's not surprising given that they're thought of as costume or "play" pieces rather than legitimate jewelry. This means that the metal itself is likely to discolor and turn green over time, and excessive wear may cause that discoloration to bleed over onto your actual ear.

The last issue with clip on earrings is one of style. For the most part, the market for clip on earrings is young girls whose parents won't let them get their ears pierced yet. As a result, the designs of such earrings are geared towards that market and that age group. For anybody past their 20s this makes finding age-appropriate clip on earrings a bit of a hunt. Mid-sized hoops I find to be a good all-purpose earring, and as a bonus the hoops also tend to be gentler than the dangling clip-ons in terms of the pressure they put on your ears.

If you're willing to hunt around you can possibly find some screw-back earrings. These were the prominent way to fake a piercing before clip ons came about. You can adjust how tight they are for slightly better comfort. Since it's a vintage way to have fake earrings they're also easier to find in more grown up styles. But the pinch is still there if you're wearing them long term, and I've found they are often heavier than clip ons, which can require you to tighten them more than you might otherwise. It's all a mixed bag in the end.

CHAPTER SEVEN

BANISHING BODY HAIR

Much of cross dressing is about creating things that most men don't have naturally: long hair, breasts, hips, etc. There is one area that both genders have to contend with in the realm of removal, but it's something that men have to deal with to a greater degree: getting rid of body hair. To be fair, it's very much a societal construct that smooth skin is feminine, and there's nothing stopping even a cisgender woman from letting her body hair stay right where it is. However, fair or not, the general societal consensus is that body hair is not feminine. And speaking personally, there are few things that can kill my own sense of femininity faster than to run my hands over my own body and come across hair where I want things to be smooth. If you're anything like me, the feel of body hair is deflating and demands action, and thus it's likely to become an ongoing battle for as long as you choose to dress.

Of course, it's worth pointing out that it's hardly a requirement that men dressing as women shave their bodies bare. Those not going out in public may not even feel the need to shave their faces smoothly. Heck, if you really just want to wear a dress and go out in a full beard then go for it! As with so many of these things, it can vary depending on how dressing fits into your life and what you hope to experience or express by it. However, for most of us, part of feeling feminine is the banishment of as much visible body hair as possible. Removal isn't required, though leaving it in place can severely limit clothing options if you don't want it getting noticed. If you're not going to shave the hair from your legs then you'll be forced to wear some form of pants or an ankle-length skirt if you don't want hair to show. You can try to cover up with pantyhose, but in my experience the dark and coarse leg hair of men shows through even the most opaque hose, at least a little. Tights or leggings can do the job a bit better, but that's a fashion avenue that isn't for everybody (myself included). Leaving chest hair in place is similarly limiting, as it eliminates the option of anything with a lower neckline. To put it simply, the best way to free yourself up to be able to wear any clothes you wish is to get rid of hair altogether.

This is, sadly, easier said than done. There are number of options out there, each with their own advantages and drawbacks. For most of my dressing life, my primary method has been shaving. It's worth noting that I'm fortunate in that I don't have a great deal of body hair in the first place. When it comes to body shaving I only have three areas to worry about: armpits, legs, and chest. My chest hair is sparse at best, so that's always been the easiest to deal with. Armpits also aren't difficult in terms of the actual shaving. However, I did find that I had redness and irritation for quite a while. Ultimately, I switched my deodorant to an aluminum-free "naturals" variety and that seemed to clear everything up and keep it that way, though darkness in the pits stuck around for almost a year before clearing up for good. So really, the pits and chest are quick and easy as far as the actual hair removal goes. The legs, however, are a bit more of an endeavor.

A smooth body can help you embrace your femininity all the more.

The idea of removing body hair is frightening to many dressers, because they fear it will be some kind of give-away when they are in boy mode. We tend to be afraid that if we wear shorts, or take off our shirts at the beach in the summer, and there's no body hair, people will realize that we cross dress. Like most of our paranoia-based worries, this is an overblown fear. Even if people notice your lack of body hair, their minds are not going to immediately make the leap to "cross dresser." Besides that, popular culture has done dressers a great favor; "manscaping" has become pretty prevalent. Granted, it's not as widespread as it was 5 to 10 years ago, and even then it was a minority of men who removed their body hair in this fashion, but it's still common enough that nobody really questions a hairless man the way they might have in the past. Strangers at the beach aren't going to think twice about you, largely because they have no frame of reference for how much body hair you might otherwise have. There is potential danger in people who know that you used to have heavy body hair and are now seeing your body shaved smooth. But this is unlikely to draw all that much attention unless you yourself bring it up in some manner. If somebody does say something it's best not to attempt to justify or over explain. On the off chance that someone does mention it, a simple "I just like this better" will be enough to close the conversation peacefully in most cases.

As far as actual methods for body hair removal, I'll start with shaving, as it's the method I've used the most often. First of all there is no need to invest in female-specific razors or shaving creams. Plenty of marketing dollars have created the idea of one razor for men and another for women, but there really is no substantial difference between the two. In my mind, the only reason to get anything specific to women might be to get a woman's shaving gel because it will have a more feminine fragrance (which, honestly, will be largely gone when you rinse off your legs anyway, so this is purely for personal enjoyment). You don't really even need to use a shaving gel or cream in the first place. At this point I get by with just soap and water, though if you do this I recommend soap with a high degree of moisturizer in it. I use Dove myself, as most other things will dry out my skin and make it more susceptible to razor burn.

There really is no particular trick to shaving one's legs. It's just a matter of practice. Start out with a fresh razor and a good lather and just use a slow, steady pace. The lather, be it from soap or cream, should serve as a visual guide for where you've already shaved and what you have left to get, but feel free to just feel around with your fingers for any errant hairs that might have escaped the blade. Some areas are going to be tricky to reach, notably the back of the thigh. This is part of why dressers have it a little tougher than most cisgender women, who usually don't have to shave much above the knee. The back of the thigh is also where you'll likely encounter something we don't think about: not all the hairs are facing the same way. For the most part, all the hairs on the lower leg are pointing down towards your feet, so shaving upwards catches them easily. On the back of the thigh I find, and others have confirmed that I'm not alone in this, some of the hairs are pointing up and some to the sides. Basically, I have to come at that area from several different angles to get everything. Finally, there's a good chance you'll also have to address some hairs on your feet and even your toes, especially if you're partial to open-toed shoes.

The upside of shaving is that, in my experience, it's the quickest, cheapest, and (with a little practice) least painful way to expel hair. Unfortunately, it's also the shortest lasting. You'll notice stubble showing up in only a day or two and will likely need to reshave twice a week if you want to remain smooth most of the time. So for those who are dressing consistently as more of a full-time lifestyle, this will quickly become repetitive and even frustrating. For the more occasional dresser it's probably still the best method due to its relative ease and expediency. Though I should mention that, in my experience, shaving can lead to the most irritation when the hair is growing back in, especially for those with sensitive skin. You can combat this with moisturizers and other creams, but odds are by day three your legs are going to be itching quite a bit no matter what you do.

There are other options out there besides shaving, such as depilatory creams and products like Nair and Veet. I actually used Veet primarily for almost a year, though I've since gone back to shaving, largely due to the chemical smell irritating my nose. Some other brands might be better in that regard, but I haven't felt the strong desire to go back and try. These creams do take longer than shaving, because you have to apply the cream and leave it on for a little while. However, I found the effects last longer—about twice as long actually, with notable stubble taking 4 or 5 days to show up. The added bonus is that the hairs don't all come back at once as happens with shaving. The regrowth tends to be a bit more staggered and results in less irritation overall. As with pretty much everything, I advise getting the formula for sensitive skin. You'll want to try just a small patch at first, because some people have bad reactions to the chemicals. Even if that patch works out well, be sure that you don't leave it on longer than directed (10 minutes max for most products) because then you'll end up with some nasty reactions no matter what. And exercise extreme caution in applying these sorts of products to any body part more personal than your legs, as the chances of a bad reaction are exponentially higher.

Epilators are an interesting alternative, at least on paper. An epilator is basically a high-speed set of electric tweezers. This means that rather than cutting the hair off at the surface level like shaving does, it actually pulls the hair out completely. The benefit is that it takes longer for the hair to grow back, even more so than with the creams, and the hairs that do come back are likely to be thinner and finer. Also, I haven't experience the same sort of itching scratchiness that I get when shaved hair starts coming back in. The problem, however, is that it hurts, and anybody who tells you otherwise is a masochist. Think of how much it hurts to pluck a single hair with a pair of tweezers. Now realizing you're doing that for every hair on your body that you remove with this thing.

For me, the epilator has an even bigger issue than the pain, and that is how long it takes. Because the device needs to get a grip on the hair and pull it, you can't just glide along your leg like you can with a razor or when scraping off Veet. You have to go slow and steady, wincing in pain the entire time. And you'll often find you have to go over the same area several times to get all the hairs. It's not a pleasant experience. That said, for those who want to keep their legs bare all the time it's a viable option. As mentioned, the hair comes back a bit finer so keeping up with this makes it a little faster and less painful each time. However, if either choice or circumstance makes it likely that your body hair will come back in full force before you remove it again, I would avoid this choice. It's at its most painful when yanking out thick and fully-established hairs.

One other word of caution from my experience with these devices: some of the hairs would grow back but not stand up as normal. It was as though they were just beneath the first layer of skin. They weren't quite ingrown because there was no excessive irritation and I could still clearly see the hairs, but they wouldn't stand up to be caught by the epilator or even a razor. As a result, I found myself digging these errant hairs out with tweezers or a needle. I don't know if this is a common issue or if I just had an unlucky reaction, but it was the final straw for me with epilators. I haven't gone back to them since.

In a similar vein to the epilator is waxing. This is one process on which I'm somewhat torn. While it is as painful as the epilator (it's also yanking out the hair, after all) it's much, *much* faster. So, in a way, it seems like the best of both worlds. The pain is still there but it's short-lived, akin to ripping off a really big bandage, and you get the benefits of longer lasting results with finer hair. Where this gets tricky for dressers is in the application. There are plenty of at-home waxing kits, but it's easier for women to use these. As mentioned before, most women don't have to deal with hair above the knee, so they can get to all the areas they need to wax with relative ease. That omnidirectional hair on the thighs is where things get difficult for men. And, of course, it's even trickier if you intend to wax your rear end. Trying to apply wax to that area properly is very difficult for those of us who are working alone. If you can get a partner willing to help then things get easier, but not all dressers have that.

There are also pre-waxed strips which can make doing it yourself easier, and it's certainly less messy than a waxing kit. Just keep in mind that you'll be dealing with more body hair than a woman, so a single box of strips isn't going to get rid of all of it; you'll need to buy several just to do your legs. There will be some difficulty in getting everything and you'll have to hit a few errant hairs with either a razor or tweezers, but the pre-waxed strips work surprisingly well overall.

Depending on where you live there may be an option for getting professionally waxed. But as a regular means of hair removal it's going to add up in cost quickly in a short period of time. It can even be a hefty expense as a one-time thing depending on how much of your body you intend to get waxed. Not to mention that going to get one's legs waxed is a level of exposure that many dressers simply won't be comfortable with. Luckily, the prevalence of "manscaping" means you won't really get many questions. And even if the waxer asks your reasons for doing it, it's just to make conversation and I can assure you that they've heard it all by now. I ended up chatting to my waxer about doing drag shows as she was working. I do highly recommend a professional wax at least once, if only as a special treat. I found it to be a pleasant experience overall (pain was surprisingly minor and in short bursts) and the results were simply wonderful. If I could afford to keep up with professional waxes it would be my preferred method, but unfortunately it is a bit of a luxury service. It's also worth pointing out that some places that do waxing either won't see men at all, charge more for men, or offer much more limited services for men in terms of what parts of the body they are willing to wax. So do your homework before booking an appointment. In my case I have to drive two hours to find a wax specialist who will work on a man without restrictions.

There are options for more permanent hair removal out there, but they are quite expensive and generally more applicable to those of us who make the decision to live more or less full-time in female mode or otherwise transition genders. I can't really comment on these options as they aren't something I myself have any experience with. However one chooses to tackle it, body hair is something that we all have to deal with. We're either taking it off or covering it up, and either way it can quickly become the bane of a dresser's life.

A NEW HEAD OF HAIR

In my experience most dressers have one piece of their attire that brings it all together. This item is the true essential that makes them feel more properly transformed than any other single thing. For some it might be lipstick, or pantyhose, or the right pair of shoes. For most of my dressing life it was the hair. All the rest of it is important, from the clothes to the makeup, but there's something about putting on a wig with a feminine hair style that just makes it all feel complete.

In a way that's odd, considering that I've had naturally long hair off and on over the years. One would think that I'd be able to feel feminine simply because of that, but I just didn't. (Well, maybe the few times my ex-wife gave me a French braid, but it wasn't quite the same.) It's not just about hair length, of course. It's also about style. When my hair was long I didn't have it cut into any kind of feminine hairstyle. It was just sort of there, usually pulled back into a ponytail. But a wig, even one that was shorter than my natural hair, made me feel instantly more feminine. Beyond the look of it, there's something about flipping it out of my face, tucking a loose strand behind my ear, or feeling the way it bounces on my shoulders that just seals the deal for me when it comes to feeling feminine.

I suppose in a way it goes back to the make-believe of childhood. What was the most important costume piece when you were playing pretend? It was always whatever went on your head. You weren't really a cowboy until you had on a cowboy hat. You weren't really a firefighter without the red helmet. You weren't a princess without a tiara. You could be missing all of the costume pieces from the neck down, but as long as you had the right item on your head then you were that thing. For me it was very much the same thing with putting on a wig. For most of my dressing life I thought that without feminine hair I was a man in a dress. With it, I was a woman. This isn't as much the case now since I've started experimenting with blurring the masculine/feminine line a bit more. But we'll come back to this in the last portion of the book.

Of course, actually buying wigs isn't always the easiest process. I think, more than any other product, it's something you really can't know will work until you're actually wearing it. Once you figure out your sizing you can figure out most clothes well enough to get by. But hair is a whole different game. Something that looks great in a picture or on a stand could look just plain wrong on you. That's why women's haircuts are so much more involved than men's. Men can go into a salon and just say "shorten it up." A good woman's haircut is customized to fit her face and features, and with wigs the same level of attention is needed.

As with most dressers, my early wig purchases were done over the Internet. And honestly, I got lucky. I bought three wigs and came away with one that worked really well (chin-length, ginger), one that was ok (wavy, long, blonde), and only one that didn't work on me (dirty blonde with bangs and highlights). Given my experience with wig buying since then, I know that this kind of success rate is a decent one if you're not actually trying them on before you buy.

There are a few things to take into consideration when buying a wig. First, realize that you get what you pay for. If you grab a bagged wig from the Halloween aisle at the local drug store for $10 then it's going to look like a cheap costume piece. The least I've paid for a decent looking realistic wig is $30 (which was on clearance, so it normally would have been more like $50), but truly high-quality ones can cost hundreds, especially if they use real human hair. Of course, paying more doesn't increase the chances that the style is going to actually look good on you, it just means the quality of material should be better. Keep that in mind before slapping down a week's pay on a human hair wig.

There's also the issue of color. One of the fun things about wigs is the ability to have a hair color besides the one we were born with. However, this also can make things trickier. Going with a hair color in stark contrast to your natural color increases the chances that it's not going to look right on you, or at least that it's not going to look natural. (Something can still look good and fun without fooling anybody into thinking it's your natural hair; one of my favorite wigs is dark purple.) Another consideration when you get a wig that doesn't match your normal color is your natural hair showing through. This is mostly an issue for dark-haired dressers that are trying to go blonde. If you can't afford a top tier product then there will be parts where your natural hair shows through gaps in the wig. The wind could blow the wrong way and suddenly there's dark hair showing under your blonde wig. Also, if you have even a miniscule bit of sideburn, then it's almost a given that your natural hair will show a little at the temples. You can use a wig cap to mitigate the issue somewhat, but personally I've always found them rather bothersome. They can slip and often gave me headaches from the continuous pressure they put on my skull. When I had longer hair I accepted them as the only way to keep my natural hair contained, but these days I really don't bother with them. The added bonus of getting a wig close to your real hair color is that it can extend the life of that wig. Over time wigs simply become less full. Brushing them out is going to pull out hairs and they don't grow back. But if the hair that's showing through a thinning wig is the same color as the wig itself then you'll get away with holding onto it for a bit longer. It's a nice thing to keep in mind for the dresser on a budget.

Beyond color, there's also the question of styling. One of the natural appeals of any given wig is that they tend to come pre-styled for you. You may find, however, that you want to make some adjustments, or try to bring some life back to a wig that is losing its bounce. When you do, you're going to want to avoid heat-based products like curling irons or flat irons or really anything that plugs into the wall. Unless it's a human hair wig it is likely to be melted by the heat, and even a human hair wig can be easily damaged by the improper use of heat. Instead, I recommend simply wetting the wig. A wet (and ideally clean) wig will be easier to reshape. You can comb the part into a different spot, for instance, and then when it dries the part should stay where you put it. If you have a wig with curls or waves that are losing their bounce I recommend getting some old-fashion sponge rollers. Again, just wet the wig, then set the rollers and take them out when the wig has dried. I've gotten extra life out of a number of wigs this way.

As much as buying wigs online is a roll of the dice, those living in more rural areas may have no choice. However, if there is a dedicated wig shop or a year-round costume shop with a good wig selection, then I really can't emphasis enough that you should go in and try things on. This is one industry that is well acquainted with the dressing community, and I can guarantee that you will not be the first man coming in to have a feminine wig fitted. If you're still worried, wait until October and everybody will assume it's for a Halloween costume. Because, as I said, until you see it on you don't really know for sure if it's going to work for you. So if you don't want to end up with a closet full of Internet-bought wigs that aren't right for you, I highly recommend making a field trip to a wig store if there is one in your surrounding area.

Of course, if you're on the bolder side of things you may find yourself wanting to do something more feminine with your actual hair. This was something I thought about idly for a very long time and I only recently pulled the trigger on it. The major thing that held me back was the consideration of how visible I wanted my gender-fluidity to be if I wasn't going full-on feminine presenting. For a long time I put that dividing wall between my masculine and feminine sides and it's only more recently that I've let that wall come down and allowed my "standard" presentation to mix these two sides.

The decision to get to the hair that I now enjoy (or, more accurately, completely adore) was several steps. It started with just going lax about maintaining the short style I'd had for some time. I didn't do this with any specific agenda, but I felt I was ready for something different. I just let my hair grow while I tried to figure out what I was going to do with it. And I dragged my feet long enough that I realized I could do something a little bit more feminine or gender bendy with my hair. I turned to my friend Karin, a professional hairdresser who I know through my performances with the Green Mountain Cabaret. I knew I could trust her to work with me since I only had a vague idea of what I was after. She trimmed up the sides and back and shaped the top so that it hung down a bit. And I loved it.

I'm not sure I ever loved my hair as much as I started to here.

About six months later I went back to get some color put in my hair. This was also something I'd thought about but was hesitant to pull the trigger on. But then I tried something with temporary hair color and I rather enjoyed the effect. I took the hair that is effectively the top layer and combed it out of the way and then colored the hair under that. The result was that when I combed that top layer back over, the color was more of an undercurrent, sort of a veil or waterfall effect. I debated between three colors at first (pink, purple, and turquoise) and was leaning towards purple. When my daughter put her vote in for turquoise I did a quick Internet search to see purple and turquoise together and decided that was the way to go for.

I went to Karin again for the color and she did not let me down. She even let me in on a trick I probably would have taken an embarrassingly long time to think of on my own. Combing my hair in the direction I normally do gives it the veiled effect I mentioned. But combing it the other way puts the color on the top layer and really lets it shine, if that's what I'm feeling. I'm not sure I can stress enough how much I love my hair right now. It's probably more than I've ever loved my hair in my entire life. I know it wasn't something I was ready for earlier in my life. Now, though, I couldn't be happier. And the result is that at this point I almost never wear a wig unless I'm cosplaying as a specific character (I've cosplayed as Poison Ivy and Wonder Woman, for instance, who have pretty specific hair requirements). And if I want to present more masculine I just tuck the hair up under a hat and I'm set.

FINDING A VOICE

Dressers, by our natures, obsess over the visual: looking pretty, looking feminine, having the right gestures and posture and all of that. However, the way you look is not the only way in which you can be judged as feminine or masculine. There's also the way that you sound. The voice is the giveaway point for many dressers, either because they fail to cover their masculine voice at all or because they do so in an unconvincing fashion.

I'll start by saying that those who have any kind of background in singing are going to have an easier time at this. Fully-trained singers will probably have no trouble developing a feminine voice, but any background in vocals is helpful. For myself, I sang in school choruses from elementary all the way through high school. While I believe I'm a decent singer, I'm not phenomenal, nor do I have any proper vocal training. But I'm still able to pull from what I know about my own voice and its capabilities to find a feminine voice.

First, it's probably best to set aside the goal of a truly convincing, 100% feminine voice. Very few of us can ever achieve that. At the very least it'll never sound totally convincing to our own ears. Most of us have to just settle for being more feminine than our normal everyday voice. So it'll be more feminine by comparison but not necessarily feminine in and of itself. The second thing is to remember that to truly feminize your voice it's not just a matter of pitching your voice up, though that's obviously a major part. Women also have a different rhythm to their speech that is essential to emulate if you don't want to sound like a guy.

But let's start with the pitch. The main thing to avoid is talking in falsetto. This is a singing term for when a singer (usually a man) flips into a much higher-pitched way of singing that is also much breathier than usual. Some singers who do this include Michael Jackson, Justin Timberlake, and Smokey Robinson. For a point of reference for how falsetto sounds when trying to use it in *speech*, refer to any Monty Python sketch where the members of the troupe play women. That high pitched, almost screechy voice is a form of falsetto. While I have to grant that in the Monty Python example they are deliberately trying to sound grating, it still serves to illustrate how poorly falsetto works as a way to approximate feminine speech. The best case scenario is that you'll sound like Miss Piggy, which doesn't really work if you're not covered in felt.

So instead it becomes a matter of pitching your voice up as much as you're able to without flipping into falsetto. This will be a matter of practice, and you need to stay low enough that your voice doesn't begin to sound strained. A good way to develop your voice is to find some songs by female artists that you can sing along with. Be careful to not get overly ambitious, and stick to singers with somewhat deeper voices. Annie Lennox is a good choice. I like to sing songs by P!nk myself. Though she does tend to go out of my range in the chorus part of many songs, I can still sing the verses at the correct pitch. Elle King ends up being similar for me as well. Just don't try to sing with Mariah Carey—you'll kill yourself.

The other thing singing will do is help you get comfortable with a more melodic mode of speech. When women speak they are more lyrical and flowing both in the quality of their voices and in how they phrase sentences. By contrast, men tend to be more forceful and blunt in the way they say things. Singing can help develop that more flowing way of speaking. And of course, observation and imitation will also be to your benefit here. Listen to the women in your home life or at your work and try to flat out imitate them at first (though not so they can hear, that might get a little weird). Failing that, just try imitating women on TV or in movies. Once you get the hang of it you'll be able to start adapting the way they speak with your own words and it will gradually become less of an imitation and more a discovery of your own feminine voice.

It is going to feel unnatural for a time but if you practice at it that will stop being the case. I'm to the point that I have to truly force myself to use my male voice if I'm in full dress, because it just feels strange to do. And for the record, I've never experienced accidentally slipping into a feminine voice when I was in male mode, which I know is a concern for some.

SITTING LIKE A LADY

Sitting down is one of those things that everybody seems to take for granted, to the point that many of us don't realize how engrained in us is a "masculine" or "feminine" way of sitting. That is, until we try to alter it. What I'm talking about here is not necessarily generic "proper" posture. Rather, I'm addressing the general ways in which men tend to sit and how they need to be prepared to alter that in order to sit in a more feminine fashion.

There are two main issues for men when we sit down. The first is that we tend to slouch. We either slouch forward, curving our backs into a sort of "C" shape, or we over lean against the backing of the chair. If this lean back was with our backs flat against the chair that would be one thing, but most of us tend to lean at more of an angle, with really only our shoulders and upper backs touching the backing of the chair while our hips and butts are closer to the edge of the seat. A feminine way of sitting can't be accomplished when such a slouch or a lean is being used.

Believe it or not, sitting like this can become second nature.

What you want to try and do is to sit up straight and have your shoulders rolled back. Your spine should be slightly arched so that your backbone is in more of an "S" shape.

This does a few things. It will push your (likely padded) chest forward and emphasize your breast area, while also giving a more feminine curve to the lower back and rear end. In terms of what to do with your hands, I advise against putting them on armrests (if they're present). Folding your hands in your lap is a good way to keep them from wandering off. When we lose track of things like our hands it becomes easier to start to slip into more habitual and masculine ways of sitting or moving because we tend to default to what's comfortable.

The other issue besides the shape of the back is the position of the legs. Most women have been conditioned from years of wearing skirts and dresses to keep their knees together, while men just don't have that conditioning. While most men don't necessarily sit in some obscene, fully splayed fashion, very few are used to keeping their knees locked together. As a dresser, even if you're wearing jeans or slacks rather than a dress or skirt, you'll still want to keep your knees together. This look is simply more inherently feminine than parted knees, even if the part is slight. Similar to keeping the knees together is what you should be doing with your feet. You'll find that it's easiest to keep your knees together if your feet are also being kept together, or possibly even crossing one over the other at the ankles and tucking them under the chair (which is a good trick if you are tall and find yourself in a chair that's a little shorter than the ideal).

Bringing up crossed feet leads us into the issue of crossed legs. Both men and women cross their legs but the way in which they do so is inherently different. For the most part, when a man crosses his legs he is resting his ankle on the opposite knee. The resulting pose is completely unworkable if you're in a skirt or dress, and even if you're in some kind of pants or leggings it's not a particularly "lady-like" way to be sitting. Women tend to cross their legs more fully so that one knee is directly above the other. If this is something that you're not used to doing, it's going to feel strange, possibly even forced and unnatural. Like so many of these things it's going to take practice. You may even find that you're not able to do it, if your legs are either too thick (from muscle or fat) or you simply lack that level of flexibility in your legs. If that's the case it may be best to forego leg crossing in favor of crossing your ankles as mentioned above. I do recommend keeping at it though. It took me a little time to really feel natural crossing my legs in a feminine fashion, but now it's become my default pose to the point that if I'm out of dress I have to really think about it if I intend to cross them in the traditionally "masculine" fashion.

CHAPTER EIGHT

THE BLESSING OF A BOSOM

In the pursuit of a feminine appearance, male cross dressers are mostly adding onto what they normally have. We truly *need* makeup, because unlike cisgender women we lose almost *all* feminine facial aspects without it. We need wigs, for style if not length. Yet there's something more basic, more fundamental to a feminine appearance that men lack: breasts.

Faking breasts is one of the first things a dresser has to figure out how to do. First, there's the inherent femininity of them. Having the bulge of a chest is highly reassuring for men wishing to appear feminine. This is because it's perhaps the single, most obvious things women have that we don't. And the human instinct says if it has breasts then it's a woman. Of course, reality teaches us that some women are flat chested while some men really need a bra, but the conventional wisdom of "breasts = woman" is still the default mindset for most people.

Beyond just feeling feminine, there's a practical issue as well. Women's clothes are designed and cut with a bust in mind. A man attempting to wear women's clothes and not doing something to enhance the bust line just doesn't look quite right because, regardless of whether anything else gives the truth away, the clothes simply won't lay correctly on the body. Without something to fill out where the breasts should be a dress may be able to create an androgynous appearance, but a truly feminine one will prove elusive. The fact that many breast cancer survivors who have had mastectomies make use of false breasts to restore some sense of lost femininity proves the point of how important a bust can be.

In the early days I started doing what I suspect most dressers who are still finding their footing do: awkwardly stuffing a bra with whatever I could find. This is a truly beginners "solution" and it's not something I'd ever recommend sticking with long term. Because no matter what I used (usually balled up t-shirts or boxers) there would inevitably be lumps where things should be smooth. Beyond that, the breasts appeared to just jut out from my body rather than having a natural flow to the curves. I've heard about, though have not personally seen, dressers who claim that high grade balloons filled with water can work quite well in terms of properly filling out a bra, since they have the correct weight and also a certain bounce to them. Angling them so that the knot is where the nipple would be can even give that impression. However, the drawback of potential puncture is obvious. I've received letters from others who claim mixtures of various viscous products besides just water work better, but then you risk ruining your clothes if they puncture instead of simply wetting them. Again, this isn't anything I have firsthand experience with myself.

To do it right you really need to get breast forms, and odds are that you're going to end up spending a bit of money on them. That's not necessarily a requirement, but as with wigs you get what you pay for with these things. Cheaper ones are usually made of some manner of foam. And the foam ones do a surprisingly good job of it for the cost (which tends to be about one-fourth of what silicon ones will run you). They can actually have a good shape and form to them, but these less expensive options have notable disadvantages when it comes to feel and weight. Since the foam is lightweight, it may fill out the bra but it's not going to have the proper heft and bounce that a real breast would have. They'll also be very obviously fake to the touch if felt by others (that's not a concern for all of us, but it depends on what you're getting up to while in dress).

Silicon, latex, or breast forms of similar materials are going to cost much more but overall look much better. They will have the proper weight and feel to them, and you can also get them in much more realistic flesh tones. They are an investment, and I do recommend taking very good care of them. My first pair lasted me a number of years, but admittedly I was rather rough on them. Because I couldn't get an adhesive that seemed to hold them on, and at the time I was wearing outfits that didn't really work with bras on a semi-regular basis, it wasn't uncommon for me to duct tape them to my chest. The pain to myself was minimal, but the damage to the breasts over time was much more noticeable.

My current pair I've taken much better care of. I also ended up going up a rather significant size with these, though that was somewhat unintentional. My first pair were slightly concave on the back side. Since I was flat chested that meant that the D cup forms only really bumped me up to a C. On my second pair I went DD only to realize that they were completely flat on the back and the jump in chest size ended up being more noticeable than I had planned. I get away with it, mainly because of my height. They still appear large, but not comically so.

This brings up the issue of size. Since cross dressers have an instinct to overdo the things that we believe will make us more feminine, most of us tend to gravitate to a larger cup size. However, it's very important that your cup size be justified by your body type. If you're 5'6" and weigh 130 pounds then you probably shouldn't be trying to upstage Dolly Parton. If you're unsure of what size is actually going to look good on you this is where those cheaper foam forms can come in handy. You can use the cheaper option to try out a few different sizes before spending money on the higher quality models.

I suppose it's worth touching on the idea of holding breasts to your body with some form of adhesive. I mentioned earlier using duct tape, and while that did the job it also did a number on my first pair of breasts. There are things like spray or roll-on adhesives out there that some dressers will swear by, but personally I've never had any luck with such products. Eventually, I did spring for a medical-grade adhesive that was recommended to me by multiple sources. But it just never held things onto me very well, no matter how much time I gave it to dry. The breasts would still slip and it left a tacky residue on the breasts and on my skin. I tried it on smaller things, thinking that maybe my breasts were just too heavy, but even that didn't give me what I'd call a positive result. I'll grant that it's possible I just got a bad batch of the adhesive, but the experience was negative enough that I've kind of given up on the idea.

Once you've actually gotten a nice, new, shiny pair of tits there's something else that you'll have to address: cleavage. Depending on the outfits you're wearing it may not be enough to simply have a feminine silhouette. If you have anything with a low-cut neckline the lack of any real cleavage is going to be a give-away and generally look a little bit off. Without proper cleavage it's obvious that the breasts are disconnected and not part of your actual body. So that means you have to fake cleavage. I've known some performers or models who use makeup to give the illusion of cleavage through shadows, but like many performer tricks that works better from a distance under harsh stage lighting than it does up close. In my own experience there's really only one way to do this convincingly that stands up to close inspection: squish whatever excess skin or fatty deposits you have in your chest together and hold it there.

The first part is easy enough, unless you're too skinny to have much to push together (and if that's the case you should be going with smaller forms to match a smaller overall body anyway). The trick when faking cleavage is keeping that forced chest fat or excess skin together once you've got it in place. There are garments out there, similar to normal bras in their overall design, which claim to hold it all in place. I haven't used these products myself so I can't attest to how well they work or how comfortable they are, though I've seen a few glowing recommendations from other dressers. For the majority of the time that I've dressed, I've just opted to tape my cleavage in place. I keep everything pressed together by putting a piece of heavy duty tape at the nipple level. It's not all that uncomfortable to go about in, but it does hurt to remove, particularly if you've had it on for a while. Keep in mind this is tape being applied only to my own body, *not* to the forms. The one big disadvantage to this technique is the same as using tape to hold a tuck: sweat. If you're out dancing or it's just a hot night out you're probably going to sweat enough that the adhesive of the tape will give way.

For this reason I've recently started exploring the world of adhesive bras. It's been a bit like when I stopped using tape for my tuck and just got a gaff to do it properly. These bras are exactly what they sound like: they stick to each breast area and then you pull them together and they clip in the front to create cleavage. Now, this will create some amount of bust as well, but my own recommendation would be to get an A cup adhesive bra and then just use forms over that as you would normally so that the bra is simply creating the cleavage. I've had some folks recommend layering a couple of these bras on top of each other to create both cleavage and a bust that doesn't require a bra to keep up, but frankly I haven't had the money to buy multiple adhesive bras to try this out as yet. Regrettably, much like with tape, the adhesive will start to give overtime, especially if you're sweating, though it does last much longer. So the main thing you gain by going this route is comfort as this is immeasurably more comfortable than using duct tape.

THE STRUGGLE FOR CURVES

As men trying to appear feminine we can stress over makeup and hair styles or even body hair, but really the biggest clear difference between what we are naturally and what we're trying to appear to be is more fundamental than that: it's the silhouette. For most people the go-to image of a feminine silhouette is shapely; it has curves that men simply don't have. There's the curve of the bust, which I've talked about. But there're also the curves of the hips and the butt, which is yet another area that, as men, we have to work on in order to appear more feminine.

When it comes to lower body curves there are two basic approaches for combating the typical male lack of hips. You can either cinch the waist in or pad the hips out. Which option you go for is going to be a matter of personal preference and also some experimentation for what looks best on you. You can certainly use a combination of the two if you really want to go big with it, though that can border on a drag queen-style of overdoing it.

Most of my own experience is with cinching the waist in so I'll start there. There are two devices used for this: corsets and waist cinchers. Both do essentially the same thing: they tighten around the waist to make it smaller, which will create a nice curve for your hips that wouldn't be there otherwise. The difference between a simple cincher and a corset is really cosmetic. Corsets are designed to not only cinch your waist in but also to be pretty. They're meant to be seen and feature visibly pleasing fabrics and patterns. Cinchers do the same thing but have a much more utilitarian look. They're the cinching equivalent of granny panties: they get the job done but they're not meant to be shown off. As a performer, I tend to favor corsets myself.

Corsets, due to their more flamboyant visual nature, can get expensive. This is especially true of steel bone corsets, which you really need in order to get the job done properly. Be cautious of inexpensive corsets, as they may only have the appearance but not the strength to actually do the cinching. If you see a corset for less than $50, check what material the boning is made of. If it's plastic then it's going to warp and lose shape almost immediately and will never cinch you in the way you want. Even if it says the boning is steel, check the fine details as to whether it's flat steel or spiral steel. Flat steel does the job right; spiral steel is only slightly better than plastic and really isn't good enough. The less flattering cinchers, by contrast, tend to do the same job for less money and there isn't the risk of being suckered in by something pretty but ineffective. It is worth noting that if you're willing to take the time to shop around online you can find affordable corsets that still work well. Just be prepared to do a little leg work.

There are numerous styles of corsets and I personally favor an underbust corset. These are ones that stop just before getting to where the breasts would be. There are plenty of gorgeous overbust corsets that are designed to cover the breasts as well, but the problem is that they're not made with breast forms in mind. They're designed to work with breasts that are naturally attached, and for that reason they're not especially suited for dressers who are using breast forms. An underbust corset allows you to wear a bra and have your breast forms in place, giving you the upper curves to compliment the lower ones you've just created.

Done up for a Rocky Horror *party, with the hourglass figure courtesy of a corset.*

Actually putting a corset on can be a bit of a trick, especially if you're working alone. There is going to be lacing in the back that needs to be tightened up and tied off, and this is easier to do if you have somebody doing that work for you.

Depending on how you lace it up, it is possible to do on your own but it will take a bit of practice. Also, be cautious when tightening to not cinch too much. You still need to be able to take a full, deep breath. If you find you can only get about half a lungful of air then you've tightened the corset too much and you need to loosen it a little bit.

As much as I love the look that corsets give me, I generally only wear them for photo shoots, shows, or special occasions. I've had people ask me about wearing them all day long under male clothes, or even for back support. This isn't something I really recommend. While it is true that it will force you into a straight posture, there are other things at play that will cause you discomfort. I'm mainly referring to the boning. In my experience, wearing a corset (and especially sitting down in one) for an extended period causes the boning that keeps the corset in shape to dig into my pelvic region. This is not as severe with a simple cincher.

If corsets or cinchers clamping down your waist aren't your thing the other option is to add padding to the hips. If you hunt around you'll probably find various undergarments with built in padding for sale online, with pads either in the hips, butt, or both. While I won't claim that none of these work, my own experience is that the padding either doesn't do much or doesn't look convincing. Taking a generic pad and trying to have it properly work on your unique body is a dice roll at best, and one that doesn't usually pay off. Not to mention the fact that most of us need more padding than the fairly sparse bit that is stuffed into these prefab garments.

The best results I've ever seen with padding (short of shelling out hundreds of dollars for silicone padding similar to breast forms) is when dressers make their own. It's not all that difficult really, though takes a bit of time to do properly. The best material to use is the foam padding you'll find inside most couch cushions. Using something like an electric carving knife you shouldn't have too much trouble slicing off what you don't need and giving the cushion the shape you desire in the size you want. When it comes to keeping the padding on, things like control top pantyhose and Spanx will not only keep it in place, but also smooth out any unevenness if your shaping of the pad wasn't completely seamless. This kind of padding is actually used in the modeling industry all the time to give plus-sized models the most "ideal" curves and hourglass figure. The need to hold the pads in place with serious undergarments is the main reason I personally don't really use pads. I'm just not a fan of these types of restrictive underthings. However, I can't argue with the final results when it's done properly.

So which do you go with? Both have their benefits and drawbacks, but depending on your body type one may look more convincing than the other. You'll also find that once you've got hips, either through padding or cinching, skirts, dresses, and even pants fit better. These garments are all made with the intention of framing or sitting on the hips, so once you actually have some they just look better.

SHOWING OFF THE LEGS

In my experience everyone has one part of themselves that they feel is worth showing off. For some it's their butt, for others it's the eyes, and some people just have amazing lips.

With me it's my legs. I don't know if it's something I knew instinctively, but early on I favored short skirts and dresses over longer ones or pants. I suppose part of it is just that women are allowed to show off more leg than men and have it be considered fashionable, so it instantly feels more feminine to have my legs exposed. Beyond that, I just think I have good legs. I actually think that in general men have a leg shape that is closer to the current beauty ideal than most women do. As I alluded to earlier, men are naturally more muscular than women. This can work against us in the arms department but it also means that most of us have a naturally curved thighs from the muscles we have there. It doesn't take much to tone those into quite a phenomenal sight. For myself, I found that taking the stairs rather than the elevator to get to my job was enough to really give me some killer gams back when I was living in New York.

Of course, the question then is how does one show off the legs? For myself, I like to bare leg it in a short skirt (not scandalously short, but higher than the knee). Part of that has to do with my own mentality: if I'm going to go to all the trouble of getting the hair off my legs then I'm damn well going to show them off. That's part of the reason I rarely indulge in pantyhose, tights, or long stockings. Of course, that's me. Any of those sorts of leg coverings will still allow you to show off the shape of the leg. Some of us aren't comfortable with exposing so much skin, while for others there's just an inherent femininity to something like nylon stockings.

If you do opt to cover up your legs, there are a few options. There are full pantyhose, most of which will come with a control top that will attempt to hold in any belly pudge. These I've never cared for. I find them restrictive and in my experience the control top tends to roll down over time. But it's certainly an option for those who want it. If you're not doing full pantyhose or tights (which are functionally identical to pantyhose, just patterned rather than transparent) then you're dealing with stockings.

The first question with stockings is one of length. You can go knee-length or thigh-high. I've only ever found one use for knee-high stockings, and that's when I'm wearing knee-high boots. It allows my leg to get in and out of the boot smoother and without them the leather (or whatever imitation material my boot is made out of) will stick to my leg in a way that just feels kind of icky. (I'm pretty sure that's the technical term for it.)

Thigh-high stockings can be quite fun, but the trick there is keeping them up. A bit like the control tops, they have a tendency to start to roll down. There are two ways to combat this. You can either get stockings that have a kind of rubberized elastic on the inside of the top that basically just grips your skin and holds on for dear life through friction, or you can get a garter belt. I tend to opt for the latter. I've found that even the grippy-top stockings can start to roll down on you given enough time. But beyond that, I just think garters are fun and sexy. Something to note, and something I've seen many people mix up, is the order of dressing with stockings. You'll want to put the garter belt on and attach the stockings *before* you put on underwear. If you do it the other way around then you've trapped your underwear under the garter straps and you won't be able to get them down without having to undo the straps should you need to use the bathroom or otherwise get them out of the way. And for this reason I also recommend being sure that your panties and garter belt match in color, if not also in style. Consider them to be a set.

WORK THE BUTT

By and large people who are attracted to the female form tend to gravitate towards one of three specific regions on the body: the bust, the legs, or the butt. As a result dressers tend to fixate on these same areas as spots that we want to be sure we "get right." We've already talked about the bust and some options to show off the legs. That means that it's time to start talking about the backside.

First things first: some of us simply don't have an ass. A flat butt can happen to either men or women, but in my experience it's a more prevalent issue for men. If you don't have any shape to your rear end and it's almost a straight line from your shoulder to the heel of your foot then you're probably going to want to pad in some way. What I said about padding for the hips applies here as well. You can find some pre-padded garments but odds are that the very best shape will be achieved by making your own padding. There are also various undergarments that claim to be able to lift your rear end on their own, and some even work, to a certain degree. But keep in mind these sorts of items can only lift and emphasize what you have naturally, and if that's not much in the first place then these items won't do a great deal to remedy that. You can't lift what you don't have.

If you've got a butt that just isn't as toned as you would like it there are exercises that you can do to try and give it the shape you're after. I'll talk a little more about this later on, but the short version is that exercises like squats and lunges can help firm up the muscles in your rear end and give it more shape. Women tend to do these to try and trim fat off their behinds, but it also will help tighten the muscles there and with any luck you'll get a more rounded shape than what you might otherwise have. I should point out, however, that exercise will give you tone and shape and the whole thing overall will be fairly tight. You should probably give up on the hope of having a bouncy or jiggly butt, because by and large men just don't store their fat there the way some women do (curse you, Kim Kardashian!).

Besides exercise, there are a few basic things that dressers can do to help achieve a more feminine looking rear end. The first has to do with posture. When you're standing you want to try and have a curve to your spine that pops the rear end out a bit (this will have the added bonus to pushing your chest forward as well). High heels are your friends in this, because they tend to force you to stand in this sort of position on their own, so it's just a matter of not fighting against it. Just be sure that when you stand or walk you're not leading with your hips. In fact, your hips should tilt slightly back to give the rear end that lifted look. Lead with your chest, not your crotch.

There's another thing that dressers need to be sure that they don't do. Do not clench your buttocks together. I'm honestly not sure where the instinct to do this comes from, but I see it far too often. Perhaps it's because as men we tend to flex a muscle to bring attention to it and by clenching the butt muscles we think we're emphasizing that area. In reality you're actually giving it a very unappealing shape. First off, you may notice when you clench your butt muscles that it immediately pushes your hips forward, which is going to demolish any outward curve you might have had going. More importantly, though, it's going to flatten out the sides of your butt, obliterate any hint of roundness, and give the sides of your rear a flat, unappealing, and unfeminine look. Just don't do it.

EXERCISE

One of the more common questions I get from dressers who aren't totally happy with their bodies is: "What exercises do you do?" To this day it still surprises me to get these questions because I don't think I've got the world's best body for dressing in the first place. Like most men, I lack much in the way of hips and, at best, have a straight-as-a-board figure in most respects. That said, I also don't have an overly-masculine build, which is to my advantage when it comes to dressing. In truth, I don't do a great deal of exercise to get into the shape that I have. I've learned enough, however, in trying to maintain my body and from talking with other dressers to pick up a few tips.

Generally, there are two things that a dresser trying to get a more feminine shape has to combat: unfeminine deposits of fat and a manly musculature. The former is what I personally have a bit more experience in. Let me start by saying that there's absolutely nothing wrong with having body fat.

Whether you're cis, trans, genderfluid or whatever, there is no inherent problem with it. However, those who wish to play around with gender have a disadvantage because women and men story their body fat in different areas.

I have known a select few dressers who carried their excess weight on their hips, buns, or thighs. And if that was the case for me I honestly would be fighting to keep it rather than get rid of it. But for most of us excess fat tends to collect primarily in our gut or on the sides in the form of love handles, unfortunately. Properly sized breast forms can help offset a belly. However, love handles are my own personal bane. If they flowed outwards into the hips I wouldn't be complaining. Instead, they tend to collect just above my hip bone and then there's an indent before my actual hip starts. Rather than forming hips it becomes an instant muffin top. As a result, love handles tend to actually diminish whatever hips I might naturally have going.

There are a few ways to try and combat the fatty deposits that aren't working for you. First, there's just general weight loss through dieting, which has been the main focus of my own approach. I'm lucky enough in my genetics that I have a slim-to-average build to begin with. This means that just losing weight in general will tend to shave pounds off of any areas where my fat happens to be. I've favored Weight Watchers, as I've both seen success with it personally and feel it's a far more healthful approach than most of the diet fads that come and go. It's also relatively inexpensive. You really only need to get the guide and figure out how the point system works. Then, if you have enough discipline, you can manage on your own without meetings or coaches or apps (though those are all available if you need them). Using this system I was able to get back down to my high school weight after years of hovering around 15 to 25 pounds over that.

Of course. weight loss alone might not be enough to get the fat off the areas that are giving you trouble. Exercise is a way to more specifically target these areas. I'll be honest and say that I don't go out of my way to exercise a great deal. I do well when presented with a chance to do it, but I'm not great at creating those opportunities on my own. When I lived in New York City that gave me ample opportunity to take stairs, something that I found myself doing on my lunch break simply to pass the time. I took my lunch later than most of my co-workers and I brought my own food rather than going out or ordering anything. So that meant I was usually done eating 8 minutes into a 40-minute lunch with nobody to talk to because they were all working. So circumstances presented me with time to kill and a ton of stairs to climb, and I took advantage. However, once I moved out of New York it was more difficult because I had to really set time aside to workout.

When it comes to exercise I would emphasize that most dressers are going to want to avoid the stereotypical male workout, specifically anything involving weights or upper body focus. This has to do with the other issue that some dressers have: being muscular in a distinctly masculine way (i.e. built-up arms and upper body). Any dressers who are working out have to make a decision as to their goals. Some dressers are people who are working out anyway and are trying for that muscular build in their daily lives. That's fine, of course, but it does make a convincingly feminine appearance slightly harder and it limits clothing options because you'll likely want to cover up your biceps and any other bulked up parts. For those who are working out but are not trying to build bulging muscles it's just best to avoid weights altogether. Most exercises geared towards men are intended to not only trim fat but also build muscle, so if you don't want a muscular frame in your day-to-day life then you're probably better off opting for more traditionally "girly" workouts. This can include things like aerobics, Pilates, yoga, or Zumba.

These sorts of more generalized workouts are about burning calories and don't target any particular muscles in excess. That means that they should help you shed weight without much of the resulting muscular bulk. However, this may not be targeted enough for some if you've got specific problem areas. Anything that targets the core is going to be good at working on belly fat and love handles. And honestly, sit-ups and the like aren't a bad idea, because as long as it's not overly defined, a six-pack can still be feminine. Routines that target the abs and sides tend to be my own focus when I'm actually keeping up with workouts, which I'll admit isn't as often as it really should be.

If there is one area where it's actually ok to build up the muscles it's the buns and thighs. I've found that it's not uncommon for cisgender women to be jealous of a cross dresser's legs. The reason for this is that men generally have more muscle definition in the thigh, which gives a very nice shape to the overall leg. Some women tend to fear a shapely thigh and therefore strive for a more uniform stick leg. This actually doesn't look as good as a leg that has more shape and curve to it as it meets the hips. This is why walking the stairs so much did wonders for my legs back in New York. As I mentioned, there are also various exercises that will help build these muscles, such as squats and lunges. While there isn't much dressers can do about our lack of hips, we can give shape to our thighs and rear ends with these sorts of exercises, and those are curves which are well-worth having.

CHAPTER NINE

NAILED IT

Doing your nails is one of the most rewarding and frustrating things that you can engage in as a dresser. On the one hand (forgive the pun), it's one of the few things you can do to make yourself girly that you can look at and fully appreciate without needing a mirror. On the other hand, they are quite a bit of work not only to do, but then to undo. And this is going to be true whether you're just painting your natural nails or applying false ones.

For most of my time as a dresser it's been rare that I would take the time to do my nails at all, and even rarer that I'd do them properly. On occasion I'll slap on a couple of quick coats before a performance for extra punch, assuming I've gotten into costume and have enough time for them to dry before I hit the stage. The results are usually a bit slap-dash but since the audience isn't getting all that close I get away with it. To really do the job right takes a bit more time and patience, and as much as I love the results I rarely find it's worth it for me. But we'll come back to why that is in a bit.

You need to understand that to do your nails properly is an involved process. First you need to file your nails so that they're in a nice, uniform shape and buff them so they'll take the polish well. This is a bit of a process and it's only the early preparation. Next comes the base coat. The base coat is important for two reasons. The first is that it will help smooth out any groves in your nails that weren't eliminating by the buffing (making it doubly important if you skipped that first step). Failing to apply a base coat means that your finished polish isn't going to have the smooth uniform look that you want. There's another reason that a base coat is important: it keeps the polish from penetrating the actual nail and staining it. If you don't put on a base coat and instead start applying the colored polish directly onto the nail then when you remove it there will still be a slight stain left behind tinting your actual nail. It is almost impossible to eliminate completely. You just have to wait for it to fade with time, which can take days. This is an issue for those of us who have to go about day-to-day activities, such as a job, where we'd rather not have people notice that we've recently had polish on our nails.

Once the nails are prepped and the base coat is applied it's time to choose a color. I sometimes get asked about color recommendations, and that's a bit tricky. If you're only going out for one night you can opt to match your nails to your outfit or the colors of your makeup. If you want something you can leave on for a few days and don't want to feel restricted, then it's best to go with a basic primary color (red is especially popular) rather than some of the more outlandish neons or metallic tints that are out there. If you're stumped for a theme, syncing up with the time of year is an easy go-to. Cold blues for winter, light greens or greenish blues for spring, bright floral colors for summer, and more earthy tones for the fall. There are, of course, many options beyond just the color, such as polish with sparkles or a chrome-like finish. Feel free to experiment to find out what works best for you.

When applying the actual polish you'll usually want to do two coats. Gel polishes can work with only one but with most others the first coat is always going to look a little thin. Don't panic; the second coat will even it all out. Be sure to apply carefully, keep the polish on the nail only, and spread it about evenly. Don't glop it on in big dollops because it will take longer to dry and possibly end up lopsided or lumpy in places. You also have to be sure that you allow time for the polish to dry between every coat (including the base coat). Otherwise you'll end up gashing or smearing the work you've already done and it makes the final result less smooth and attractive. Finally, you'll want to do a top coat, which can usually be done with the same clear varnish as the base coat. A top coat helps protect the polish from the chips and nicks that are otherwise inevitable.

Now, I said I usually don't find all of this to be worth it. That isn't just because of how long it takes, but the fact that I then have to remove it all so soon after applying it. When women get their nails done they get to enjoy them for weeks, baring the chipping or flaking that can happen. Because I work at a job where painted nails on a man would raise too many eyebrows, I have to remove the polish, sometimes only a matter of hours after having applied it. Removing polish isn't an especially complicated process, just a bit of a demoralizing one when done in the same 24-hour period as applying it. To take it off, all that's required is a cotton ball and some nail polish remover. Dip the cotton ball in the remover and start scrubbing.

The other annoyance is that the more work you put into applying the polish, the more time and effort it will take to get it off. Two color coats with both a top and base coat take a bit more work to remove than just a couple of quick color coats. One way you can enjoy your work for a bit longer is to paint your toes. Odds are your feet and toes will generally be covered and out of sight in your daily life unless you go out of your way to expose them. This means that you can enjoy the fruits of your labor a bit longer, though by the same token you won't get to see and enjoy them as much as you would have with fingernails.

Of course, there's more that can be done with nails than just polish. There's also false nails to give them a length that most of us can't get on our own (either because it's impractical or because we're impatient). These can be great fun and make you feel even more feminine than nail polish alone. But they can also involve even *more* work than just the polish. To be fair, the plus side is that you don't need to buff or file your natural nails and you don't even need a base coat because there's no chance of staining the false nails and they're already perfectly smooth.

Most false nails fall into two categories: press-on and glue-on. I've never cared for press-on myself because they pop off too easily. This can be a plus for some, because it makes them easier to remove. For me, though, that is completely cancelled out by the fact that they tend to pop off when you *don't* want them to. One of the nice things about press-on nails is that you can get ones that are pre-painted and styled, whereas the glue-on ones tend to be more of a blank canvas. It's worth noting that I've had a more difficult time finding press-on nails that fit. Men's nails tend to be wider than women's due to us just having larger hands and fingers, and it's been my experience that it's easier to find larger size nails in the glue on variety.

Glue-on nails aren't really all that difficult to apply. Make sure you've selected a size that properly fits your nail, apply the glue evenly across the nail, and then just hold the false nail down onto your own nail until the glue sets. It only takes about 15 to 30 seconds. Some nails come longer than you probably want them, so they'll need to be trimmed back. This can be done before application, but I personally find it easier to clip and shape a nail that's already on my finger. Once it's on you can polish as you would normally. You can also apply polish or designs beforehand, but again that is going to require that you also shorten and shape the nail prior to application, something that never went too well for me. Perhaps you'll have more luck.

Something you should be prepared for with false nails is how much of a hindrance they are. Since you're applying the falsies to short nails (rather than growing them out over time) you rarely have the time to get used to them before you have to take them off. This means that you'll be constantly catching and tapping them against things. It's hard to put into words how annoying this feels, especially when you're not used to it. I always found typing with nails to be nearly impossible, and the nails make even holding something a slightly awkward experience because I'm trying to both not damage the nail and not damage whatever is in my hand with the nail. Even if you're not worried about damage, they just get in the way. Trying to use a phone or remote control becomes an instantly cumbersome experience. Practice makes it a little better, but odds are you'll have to take them off before you really get a chance to get used to them.

This brings up the second issue with false nails. Removing false nails can be an even more laborious process than just removing polish. I've always used acrylic nails. In the past, that meant in order to take them off I had to soak my fingers in a bowl of acetone nail polish remover (non-acetone won't do the trick). Given enough time, this basically starts to melt the nail down and you can rub and scrape off what's left. While you won't have any lingering polish or stain issues, there's a good chance there's going to be little white remnants of the nail and the glue lingering behind for a few days. Thankfully, this residue isn't the giveaway that a colored stain from nail polish is, but it's still annoying. Lately I've lost my patience with this technique and have opted to just pry the darn things off. I won't lie, this is a bit of an unnerving process. Painful might be an overstatement, but it's not a pleasant feeling and for a split second it can feel like you're prying off the actual nail (which is just shudder-inducing).

More recently I've actually experimented with growing my own nails out, more or less just to see how long I could get them before deciding I'd had enough. I'd tried that in the past with very little success but I added a new element this time: a nail hardener. A big part of what skeeves me out about longer nails is feeling them bend. A nail hardener is basically a specially-formulated clear coat that reinforces and strengthens the nails. It keeps them from bending, which reduces the chances of them cracking. Also, the shine of the clear coat makes them rather nice to look at. With my nails growing out gradually rather than suddenly being longer (like with false nails) I was able to adapt better to having them. I've gone about a month before hitting a point where

I felt like I needed normal fingers again. I kind of cycle it back around every few months these days and find it pleasant. Admittedly, I'm rolling the dice in terms of being noticed at work but I don't think nail length is as noticeable as colorful polish. Plus there are a several guitar players at my job with at least a few longer fingernails so I figure that gives me a little lee-way on the issue.

WHAT TO PACK IN A PURSE

One of the things about starting to go out in public while in dress is figuring out what to bring with you. Honestly, in male mode we have it easy. All we really need are keys, wallet, and a cell phone. We can just stick each of these in a pants or jacket pocket and go about our day. Going out as women it becomes trickier for a number of reasons.

First, there's potentially much more we're going to want or need to have on hand, for example, certain makeup items in case anything needs to be touched up or reapplied. Even if we choose to go bare minimum and strip it down to the true basics, most women's clothes don't even have pockets in the first place. Even if you're wearing jeans or slacks which do have pockets you really aren't going to want to put anything in them. Pockets on women's pants are designed to be more about look than function. As a result, most are very shallow and tight, nearly impossible to fit anything into. Even with the ones you might be able to get a wallet into, like the back pocket of some jeans, I'd still advise against it. The lump created by something in your pocket is going to break up the smooth silhouette you're trying for. So unless you're going out in a coat or jacket you won't have the usable pocket space you need. You need a purse.

If you go with a larger purse then you've made your life fairly easy. Just load it up with whatever you need and go about your day. That said, I would recommend trying to avoid needless clutter, such as too many makeup items. It just becomes annoying when you have to dig through a ton of stuff to find what you're after. But aside from organization there's no real trick to packing a large purse. If you're going for something more along the lines of "small and cute", however, then you'll have to pare it down to only what you can fit. And that's what I'm going to talk about here: the things that *every* dresser should be carrying with them.

First, there's your wallet, the one you use in your daily life as a man. I'm not saying that you have to bring the physical wallet with you, though personally I find it easier to just do that. The alternative is to take the essentials out of the wallet and put them in the purse, which may be necessary if you have a small purse and bulky wallet. So the must-haves start with your ID. This is a sticking point for many dressers, because their photo ID is going to clearly identify them as a man. This is something most of us would rather not do when we go out in dress. Whether we pass as a woman or not, we generally prefer to be treated as one and not draw attention to our masculine side. And honestly, the odds are that you won't need to present your ID unless you're on the younger side and trying to get into a club or bar. However, the circumstances that might come up that will require your ID (being carded, being involved in a traffic accident, etc.) carry heavy enough consequences that it's not worth the trouble being caught without it. There are a few states that either have or are considering a third gender option (basically an "X" catch-all for those who don't identify as male or female), but even if that option is available in your state I know most dressers aren't comfortable with that being on an official record.

The other thing you'll need from your wallet is money in some form. Many dressers I know prefer to carry cash, as nobody will ask to see ID when you pay in cash, while it's possible that ID could be asked for when using a credit or debit card. I personally still opt for cards, but that's because I hate having to guess at the start of the night how much cash I'll need; I end up either running out of money or with a bunch of bills left over. I'm just not a cash-carrier by nature, but either option is fine. Even if you're being taken on a date that somebody else is paying for you should always have money on you because you never know what might happen. It's just common sense.

Next there's the cell phone. At this point most of us wouldn't be caught dead without our phones, but it's worth emphasizing anyway. I've seen dressers leave them behind because they were taking up most of the space in a small purse. If you find yourself in any kind of jam you need to be able to reach out for assistance, and you can't count on there being a working payphone anymore. Set it to vibrate or even turn it off if you don't want to be bugged by it during the night, but always have it with you.

Now we come to the makeup, and this is where many dressers overdo it. Simply put, you don't need to put everything that you've applied to your face into your purse. There're only a handful of things you're likely to have to reapply in the course of a standard night out. The big one is lipstick. Unless you've applied a stain or something else long-lasting you will absolutely want to have the shade you're wearing on hand. Most rub off easily from so many things, the main ones being eating or kissing. Drinking can do it to, though you can mitigate the damage by using a straw rather than drinking directly from the glass (although martini or wine glasses don't really allow for this, so it depends on what you're drinking). In any case it's the single part of your makeup that you're most likely to have to reapply.

You always want to be able to do a quick refresh. Photo by Syd London.

Mascara is another thing that might need a touch up, assuming you're wearing it. As I talked about before, I opt for false lashes myself and don't really bother with mascara anymore. But if you're using it and going out for a long night you'll probably want to bring some with you. The last thing I recommend is a powder compact. This is mostly going to be needed if you're going out dancing. If and when you start to sweat, you'll want to reapply a quick bit of powder to take the shine off from time to time. The nice thing about the compact is that it'll also come with a mirror so if you can use it discretely and you won't even have to find a bathroom to touch up in.

I also recommend some form of security device. This could be pepper spray, mace, or just a simple whistle. Pick something you're comfortable having that will make you just a little bit safer. I wish this wasn't necessary, but the reality is that even if you live in a tolerant area there are always people out there who will take offense at your presence. And sometimes these people want to hurt you. You should always have some means of either defending yourself or quickly summoning help or both. Even when you're going to a place you've been to a dozen times before and know is safe, you don't know who you might encounter en route or when leaving the location. It's just not worth the risk to leave these things at home. In a pinch, your keys can also be surprisingly effective for scratching or punching with. Which brings up keys, but you know you need those right? Just keep in mind that they're one more thing that'll be taking up space in the purse and plan around that.

The last thing I recommend is the only one that I don't consider to be a must for everybody, but I want to talk about it anyway: condoms. If you are monogamously attached or know 100% that there is no chance of you hooking up with anybody when you go out then you can skip this one. But if there's even the slimmest possibility that you might get intimate I really do encourage all dressers (and really *anybody,* for that matter) to keep a couple of these handy. I had it ingrained in me from an early age: it's better to have a condom and not need it than to be in a situation where you need a condom and don't have one. Even if it's not your plan to go out and hook up, you never know who you may meet in a night or what might develop. Like the defensive items, this falls under the category of "always be prepared," though admittedly if you have to use this it's been a much better night than if you have to use the pepper spray.

SLEEPING EASY (IN GIRLY PAJAMAS)

This section's going to seem a little bit on the random side. I mean pajamas? Really? Do they honestly need their own section? Maybe not, but I'm going to talk about them anyway. Plus it gives me an excuse to share one of my favorite shopping experience stories. (That's the tease to keep you from skipping this part. I know, I'm awful.)

Feminine pajamas are one of those things I didn't really think about for a very long time. But it's something that I've dipped my toes into more recently, as I've allowed my female and male lives to bleed together more than I used to. And something as simple as distinctly feminine sleepwear has had an interesting impact on me.

Until recently, I really only ever got dressed up to go out. This wasn't because I didn't enjoy dressing up in and of itself, but I've always been of the mind that if I'm going to put on all this stuff then I should be doing something once I've finished. If I'm going to shave my legs, put on makeup, slap on a wig, and slip into painful heels I'd like to do more than just strut around the house or take a few (admittedly cute) selfies. But as I've started to explore the middle ground of my gender I've opened myself up to not having to do all of that in order to feel feminine. It's still hard sometimes. Dressing only partially can feel odd and rather incomplete to me at times.

But, in that sense, pajamas were a perfect way to explore the middle ground. With feminine sleepwear I don't have this idea in my head about how I'm supposed to look in order to wear it. It doesn't come with that kind of baggage. And slipping into comfortable but girly pajamas allows me do something that I've very rarely done when dressing: relax. Because of all the other stuff I'd always do to get ready, and because I was usually going out, I was having a terrific time but I never really relaxed. I wasn't able to unwind in anything other than male mode.

I've gotten a number of different styles of pajamas but I've found the most comfortable are usually t-shirts or tank-tops and panty or boy-short style bottoms (or fuzzy pants for colder weather). I've got a couple of button-up sets that I think are adorable but the tops twists on me awkwardly when I sleep because I tend to shift about (I'm not a thrasher but I do roll back and forth). Nighties and sleepshirts are fun, but if you move around in your sleep like I do then you'll find them riding up around your midriff come morning. You may not care, as I don't on some nights, but just be aware. I really shouldn't have to say this, but to be sure that nobody misses the memo: don't sleep in lingerie. It's made for looks not for comfort, and while it's nice to feel sexy while you sleep if that's working for you, you're going to wake up chafed and irritated with most lingerie sets.

Now for that story I alluded to. Not long ago I decided to pick up some more pajamas during a trip to Walmart (don't judge me, there aren't many options around where I live). I went in while I was on my lunch break from work to buy a couple of thrilling items like a plastic bin for storage. While I was there, I noticed they had a special on some cute pajama sets so I shrugged and grabbed two of them. At checkout, the young woman who was ringing me up got to the pajamas and said, "Oh, shopping for yourself?"

Now this should have thrown me off. As I've noted, generally clerks at stores aren't going to say anything about a guy buying girly things one way or the other. Most don't care in the first place. Even if they do, they know well enough to just ring up the purchase quickly and move on with their day. So having anything said at all was a little unusual in a general merchandise chain like Walmart. But something about her tone was friendly and open enough that with almost no hesitation I replied, "Yes I am."

She looked down at the pajamas again and smiled. Then she said, "I'm sure they'll look cute on you." After that she said something about her own favorite pajama brand. I don't know if it was one of the ones I was buying or if she was making a recommendation. It's kind of a blur because she'd just made my day with that previous comment and I was kind of in a little bliss cloud. While I do enjoy shopping, the checkout is generally a neutral experience at best. It's just the thing I have to do to take items home. And she made it the high point of my entire day with one genuine-sounding idle comment. So thank you, Walmart checkout clerk. You did more than put a dresser at ease, you lifted up my spirits in a way I can't really put into words. Bless you for it.

Part III: Philosophical Aspects

CHAPTER TEN

KNOW THE CROSS DRESSER STEREOTYPES

I've talked a little already about pop culture representations of those who dress in the clothes normally reserved for the opposite gender. These representations help to generate some of the stereotypes about cross dressers, but there are other contributors as well. Online culture has put its own stamp on what people tend to assume about cross dressers. This gives rise to even more stereotypes that you should be prepared for. To be clear, there's nothing wrong with actually falling into any of these stereotypes, nor is there anything wrong with them not applying to you. However, they are things that people are likely to presume about you upon finding out that you're a dresser, so you should be prepared to address those expectations one way or the other.

The first is one that we've already talked about to some extent: people are going to assume you're attracted to men. The prevailing image of the cross dresser is still linked to the gay community, so that's an assumption that many people will have. In a way it's easier to explain that you're not attracted to men (if this is the case) when you come out to people you know. It's actually more difficult to get others to accept that this may not be the case with you when going out or meeting people online.

These days there's also a prevalent stereotype of cross dressers being highly promiscuous and even non-discriminating when it comes to sexual encounters. This image is mostly an offshoot of the online communities. The simple fact is that most of the cross dressing community sites of notable size serve primarily to help people hook up. And even if that's not the main point of the site it will still be a prominent component. As with most stereotypes, there's some truth behind this one. Mostly it comes from that impulse of many closeted dressers to please men in order to feel feminine. I talked about it before in relation to online chat and webcams, but the same applies in real life. Many dressers, particularly those still in the closet, seek to be treated sexually by men to maximize the feeling of femininity. The side effect of this is that if you go out to a trans-friendly club or bar there is a very good chance that some of the men there will not only hit on you but be openly surprised if you don't show an interest. They tend to assume sex is the whole reason you got dressed up and went out, and anytime that's not the case they can get confused or even upset. Part of reason I eventually stopped going to trans nights at clubs in New York was that I grew sick of having to turn away the same men repeatedly. As I mentioned earlier, I'll give most people a pass the first time they hit on me. But so many won't take the "no," and it gets uncomfortable quickly.

In a related stereotype, it is assumed by many that cross dressers are sexually submissive by nature. Something you'll find both online and in person is that many men believe that if they simply show enough dominance then a dresser will do what they want. And, as with the promiscuity stereotype, there is some truth behind this. Of course, there are those for whom dressing is inherently sexual and they may be naturally submissive, and that's fine. (I'll address some of this in the next section on labels.) But there are also those who are just so desperate for attention which feminizes them that they'll give in to the dominance and pressure just to get that feeling of being feminine and desirable, even if they wouldn't normally be attracted to men. It's a trap that's easy to fall into. And between dressers who either genuinely enjoy being dominated and those who'll cave because it feeds a need for affirmation, the men who try to pressure dressers into sexual acts aren't going to go away anytime soon.

Another stereotype that is closely tied to the promiscuity issue is a surprisingly frequent assumption of prostitution. Again, as we keep seeing, this one has some roots in the online depiction of dressers and trans-folk, but this time it's more to do with pornography. Those who find dressers or trans-persons attractive also tend to be heavily into transgendered-theme porn. This is going to come up again when I talk about pop culture representations of cross dressers. I've known a few of the actresses and models who do such work from my time living in larger cities, and it's not uncommon for them to make themselves available as escorts or dominatrices, if not outright prostitutes. This is, of course, their choice, and I pass no judgment on it. As far as I'm concerned they have the right to do with their own bodies as they will. However, it does mean that in certain clubbing environments (mostly in major cities) there will be people who think that your time and your body can be bought, even if you've turned down their initial advances. I've shot down more than a few men who approached me and tried to ask me how much a "date" with me would cost them. And, much like the men who think I'm just promiscuous or submissive, they could be maddeningly persistent. They tended to think I was just holding out for a better price or that they needed to buy me a drink first and then I'd tell them a going rate.

One final stereotype to be aware of is the idea that all cross dressers are closeted. There's a general presumption that if a cross dresser was out and open that they would be living full-time as a woman and in the process of transitioning. For most people, it's hard to fathom those of us who are out but still choose to only dress on occasion. This results in an assumption of secrecy, which is usually fairly harmless. However, an assumption that you're closeted can lead to the slightly more damaging conclusion that this is a fetishistic act, something you're doing for sexual kicks. (And there we are coming right back to sex again.) People have a difficult time separating gender expressions from sexual acts. Of course, as I keep saying, for some of us this *is* a deeply sexual act, and there's nothing wrong with that. But even if it is sexual in nature you may not want to advertise it openly as such. In either case, the linking of gender expression to sexuality is something that you'll likely have to confront over and over again, regardless of whether or not it applies to you.

THE BURDEN OF LABELS

I don't know what it is about labels, but people latch onto them like a lifejacket. We act like knowing what label fits us will somehow make the world a clearer place. I've had so many questions from dressers telling me their situations and then asking for my help in figuring out which label fits them. And when it comes to those who dress as the opposite gender there is no shortage of label options: cross dresser, drag queen, transvestite, transgender, androgynous, shemale, sissy, trap, genderqueer, genderfluid, and of course about a million abbreviations (tgirl, tranny, trans, etc.). Personally, I'm largely over labels. I don't find them particularly enlightening; in fact, I often find them confining. No matter how many we come up with, they implicitly say that these are the available options and you have to fit one. More harmfully, the implication is that if you don't firmly fit one of these labels then something is wrong with you. This is why, for most of my time exploring my gender, I've just opted for "dresser" (clarifying more specifically as "cross dresser" when needed) and left it at that. It removes most of the baggage that the other names I mentioned have and just breaks it down to basics: I'm a man who wears clothes normally intended for women, my fashion crosses the gender line, therefore I cross dress. I know that many people, however, still find comfort in labels so I'm going to go through the major ones and offer some definitions and clarification. Keep in mind that the definitions I'm giving are based on my own experiences and observations, and may not be strictly "textbook" (not that there is a textbook for all of this, though that would be a help if there's an academic out there who wants to get on this). This is based on my own experience using these terms and hearing them used.

Cross Dresser: This is the most generalized term and the one that carries the least specificity. It's a pretty straight-forward, factual statement. There isn't a great deal of inherent baggage with this term and I find it quick and to the point, which is why it's the one that I've used the longest and most often to describe myself. There is no implication of the "quality" of dressing, so one does not need to body shave and do full makeup to be considered a cross dresser. The term is really for everybody. But the lack of specificity seems to bother many dressers, who want something more tailored to them. It's a term that gets used but most who use it also have a more specific additional term that they use to clarify ("part-time" vs. "full-time," for example), much like how people in the gay and lesbian community will not identify as simply "gay," but also as something more specific like "power top," "switch," "twink," "femme," "butch," and so forth.

<u>Drag Queen</u>: This is a term that is generally reserved for a male performer of some kind, generally a stage or club performer, who performs for audiences while dressed as a woman. (There is the female-to-male equivalent which is a "Drag King." Women can also be drag queens, sometimes referred to as "bio queens," though that label and performance style is kind of contentious at the moment.) While there's no strict definition of what kind of performance a drag queen engages in, the most common by far is lip synced dance routines to songs by female artists. This may involve actually impersonating a specific singer, but not always. Sketch comedy is also fairly common in drag shows, as many find humor in the exaggerated antics of drag queens. There's an assumption that all drag queens are gay. While in my experience it is of true of the majority of drag queens, it is not an absolute. It should also be clarified that not just any man who puts on a dress and prances about a stage qualifies as a drag queen. The intention of most drag queens is to maximize femininity, often to the point of camp. This can be in the form of high glamor, couture fashion,

deliberately diva-like behavior, etc. A man with visible stubble who slaps on a bra for a cheap laugh can be said to be "in drag," but wouldn't be called a drag queen.

Transvestite: In terms of the strict definition, this is interchangeable with "cross dresser." However, this one always had a more clinical sound to my ear, like a diagnosis or something you'd get treatment for. That's probably a big part of the reason I've never cared for it personally. In my experience, this term also carries with it a sexual connotation that is not present in the more neutral "cross dresser." While not *everyone* who openly identifies as "transvestite" has a sexual aspect to their dressing (Eddie Izzard being the prominent example), I've found that most who use this term choose it over other options because they dress as part of their sexual expression. *The Rocky Horror Picture Show* and the song "Sweet Transvestite" probably contributed to the assumption of a sexual component to this word. The use of the term in online communities has also heavily reinforced the sexual side, even though there may not have been one initially.

Transgender: This one can be a very broad term, yet at the same time it is often used in fairly narrow context. In truth, most of the terms and phrases I'm talking about fall under the umbrella of "transgender," which is a spectrum rather than an absolute. That said, most define the term fairly rigidly and reserve it for those who either have transitioned or are in the process of transitioning their physical sex from one to the other. Those who have actually undergone operations as part of their transition may also be labeled as a "transexual," though that term seems to be falling out of favor. These operations may include complete gender reassignment surgery (leading to the more specific "pre-op," "post-op," and "non-op" variations) but that's not a must. "Transgender" is generally applied to any person who is attempting to live their day-to-day life as the sex opposite from the one they were designated at birth, or a person who has the intention or desire to do so. Someone who uses the term transgender to describe themselves generally feels like a woman trapped in a man's body or vice versa. The degree to which they may be trying to correct what they see as a mistake of physiology will vary. Some will undergo a full physical sex change while others may opt for only hormone replacement therapy without surgery, and there are many more variations.

Tranny: On the surface this is just a shortening of "transgender" (or even "transvestite") into something that's faster to say. However, it's a term usually used to degrade and humiliate people who are transgender or who cross dress. The word itself may once have been as neutral as "transgender," but at this point it's considered an offensive and dismissive term. This is one to steer clear of in general.

She-male: We can thank the porn industry for this ugly little term. Simply put, I've never personally known a dresser or transgender individual to regularly self-identify as "she-male." Even those I've known who work in the sex industry only use the term in relation to their work, for marketing purposes. Along with "tranny," it's considered a derogatory and degrading term, one that many will take offense to if it is applied to them. Strictly speaking, in its pornographic context, it is a term with a fairly narrow meaning. It refers to people born as men, who have had selective sex change surgery (usually breast implants at a minimum) but still retain their (often functional) male genitalia. "Chicks with Dicks" is a wordier phrase used to express the same idea, and again it's one frequently used in porn.

Trap: Like "she-male," this is a term that I wish I didn't have to even talk about, but it's out there. Most often it's something that comes up in online sites that fetishize cross dressers and transgender folk. Generally it's applied to dressers who are completely convincing in their feminine appearance, until they disrobe to reveal male genitalia (think *The Crying Game*). I actually have come to hate this term even more than "she-male". That term, while degrading, I don't believe to be as outright harmful as this one. The problem with "trap" is that it perpetuates a stereotype that contributes towards violence against the transgender and cross dressing communities: the idea that we're trying to trick people. Part of the hatred towards trans people (trans women especially) is from homophobic men who have great fear and anger tied to the idea that they could be attracted to a woman and discover they've been "tricked" into being attracted to a man or otherwise having feelings they see as gay or emasculating. "Trap" very much plays into that by reinforcing the notion that trans people are playing some sort of "Ha! Gotcha! Now you're gay!" trick. It's a dangerous concept which has since been fetishized by some, but that fetishization doesn't remove the damage this idea causes.

Sissy: This is a term that used to only refer to an effeminate male, but has taken on a new life thanks to online communities and fetish pornography. It's become a highly-sexualized term at this point when used in connection with cross dressing, and those who use it to describe themselves tend to embrace that sexual connotation. It's a term used for cross dressers who are sexual submissive and often wish to have a dominant sexual partner "force" them into feminine clothing and behaviors. To be clear: the "forced feminization" is, in fact, a consensual play, with each participant accepting submissive or dominant roles in that play. There's usually an aspect of humiliation and degradation inherent in the term itself that likewise is embraced by those who use it. Unlike "she-male" or "tranny," this is a term that some dressers will apply to themselves voluntarily. However, because of its highly sexual nature, you'll want to be very careful about labeling someone else as a sissy, because if they don't consider themselves to be as such they may take great offense. Overall, it's a term that one will encounter semi-regularly online but not so much in real life, save for occasionally at fetish-focused events.

Androgynous: This is one that you won't run into as often in dressing circles, and in truth it's not *really* cross dressing. Rather, a person who considers themselves to be, or strives to be, androgynous is attempting to present as gender neutral. They will tend to wear attire and fashion that can be and is worn by either gender. This isn't something I have a great deal of experience in, but I have encountered some dressers who strive for androgyny when not flat out dressing as the opposing gender. I suppose that makes the switch less dramatic and a little smoother for some.

Gender-Fluid: This is a more recent term, and as much as I don't care for labels, it's one that I've accepted for myself at this point in my life. The idea is that someone identifying as gender-fluid isn't locked into feeling like only one gender or the other, but the one they favor can vary at any given time. It's a useful term for those who find that their gender identity doesn't seem to want to stay still for any extended period of time.

Genderqueer: This one is deliberately non-specific and one of the newer blanket terms. It denotes a person who is outside the widely-accepted perceptions of gender. This could mean that they identify as neither sex, as both sexes, as a combination of selected elements of both, or simply that they don't know what they are but do understand that they fall outside the usual male/female binary.

Bigender: It's easy to kind of get jumbled on this term and mix it up with gender-fluid, and honestly there's a bit of overlap anyway. Bigender refers to someone who feels that they are more than one gender at the same time. This differs slightly from gender-fluid, which sees a person flow from one gender to another, though some people who identify as bigender do experience this as well as the feelings of a simultaneous dual-gender.

Agender: This is not feeling a strong affinity to any gender designation. A person who identifies as agender most likely just doesn't feel an inherent pull towards any of the gender norms and is opting to just not really deal with that. Think of it like being a gender atheist.

PRONOUNS

Hand in hand with the topic of labels is the subject of pronouns. Funnily enough, the question "what are your preferred pronouns?" is one that I've only started getting asked in the last year or so. You'd think it would have come up more, but until recently I've pretty clearly presented as entirely feminine or entirely masculine. And unless somebody is the kind of person who is going to deliberately misgender you in order to be a prick about it, most will look at a person in a dress with makeup and heels and assume feminine pronouns (even if that person doesn't 100% pass). But as a greater understanding of gender begins to seep into the mainstream, and as I have gone for a more mixed presentation of myself more often, the question comes up more and more. Now, for some it's pretty straight forward. Transgender folks go with the gender they identify as. Cross dressers, by and large, will favor however they're presenting, but that does mean that the answer to "what are your preferred pronouns?" isn't as simple as "masculine" or "feminine" but rather the more complicated "it depends."

As far as your options go, there are the obvious masculine (he/him) and feminine (she/her) options we all grew up with. Some folks who identify as either agender or bigender or some other middle variant prefer a gender neutral, which gets a bit tricky. Most I've known in this category opt for "they/them" as their pronouns, because those are gender neutral. Unfortunately, they're also plural and it can really throw some of us off to refer to a single individual with plural terminology. I myself struggle with this still. In English there has yet to emerge an agreed upon gender-neutral singular pronoun. People don't go with "it" because that's just flat out dehumanizing. I've seen some attempts at getting a gender-neutral singular pronoun established with terms like zie/zir but most folks wouldn't know what to do with those terms if they heard them. So for the time being, they/them remains the best gender-neutral option.

But coming back to the issue of situational pronouns. As I said, back when I presented either completely feminine (heels, wig, skirt, full makeup, etc.) or completely masculine (flat sneakers, short hair, t-shirt, jeans, etc.) people didn't really need to ask. But now that I'm more liable to show up to events or gatherings with a feminine top, my natural hair, jeans, and masculine footwear it does beg the question. So folks don't have to ask every time I've personally opted to use lipstick as a signifier. If my friends are unsure where my headspace is at for the day, I tell them if I've put on lipstick that's feminine, otherwise masculine will be best.

Linked to that is whether people call me by my masculine birth name or my feminine chosen one. At this point (as I'm basically out in nearly every aspect of my life) I don't even bother with asking folks to switch. I advise them to just use the name that first comes to mind in their own heads when thinking of me. As a result, most of the folks who live in my town call me by my masculine name, and most of the folks who know me through burlesque and similar activities call me Vera. But for me, I'm pretty comfortable with either one. Obviously anyone with a strong preference should articulate that, because you can't assume people will do what you'd prefer without a little guidance.

POP CULTURE TRAPS

I really do feel that one of the biggest things that cross dressers have working against them is the lack of a popular culture touchstones. While there is still a great deal of progress left to be made in terms of gaining acceptance from the entire LGBTQ+ community, in many ways cross dressers are excluded from what progress has been made so far. Part of the problem is that since most cross dressers identify as straight (that is, physically male and attracted to females) and a surprisingly small portion wish to actually transition their gender full-time, most of us don't fit cleanly into the LGBTQ+ letters. But that's not really what I want to talk about in this section. My main point is that there are some pop culture points of reference that we can point to and say, "There, I'm basically like that."

There are too many gay men on TV at this point (whose influences are both positive and detrimental) to even try counting. Lesbians have people such as Ellen DeGeneres, an idol of mine due to the fact that she doesn't let her sexual preference define her, as well as shows like *The L Word*. Bisexuals admittedly have it a little tougher, but there are characters like Jack Harkness from *Torchwood* and comedians like Margaret Cho who help give some frame of reference, despite often reinforcing the promiscuity stereotype. Transgender folk have had people like Chaz Bono and Laverne Cox making strides in showing the general public that they're not so scary, and shows like *Orange is the New Black* have helped further. You can count drag queens like RuPaul in either the gay or trans camp depending on how you want to think about it, but either way it's another reference that people can latch onto.

Cross dressers, on the other hand, are sorely lacking in any kind of positive, or even properly neutral, pop culture figures. The closest would probably be British comedian and actor Eddie Izzard, who was wonderfully brave and bold in his wearing of women's clothes in his performances and also being so blasé about it. Treating it like it's no big deal is really what the world should be doing, and he does that wonderfully. However, his personal choice to primarily operate in boy mode in more recent years has made it easier for those who can't wrap their heads around cross dressing to dismiss his dressing as something he only does in his stand up specials, thus downgrading it to an aspect of a performance persona rather than a characteristic of him as a person. And please understand, I'm not criticizing him for that choice, I'm just saying it makes using him as a point of reference a bit shakier.

So without a well-known pop culture figure to refer to, the result is a very poor understanding of cross dressing from the public at large, and often even within the cross dressing community itself. Part of my early struggles with finding myself had a great deal to do with not having anything to compare myself to or judge myself against. If cross dressing is depicted at all in the popular culture it is for one of two reasons: comedic effect or implied sexual deviancy, and often both. As much as I may personally love *The Rocky Horror Picture Show*, it standing as one of the best-known depictions of transvestitism doesn't do the cross dressing community many favors due to the linking of sex acts to cross dressing. Meanwhile, a decade's worth of sit-coms like *Bosom Buddies* and films like *Big Mama's House*, *White Girls*, or *Sorority Boys* may not be actively trying to create a culture where straight men dressed as women are a joke, but unfortunately that is what happens regardless since these have been the primary pop culture depictions out there for a very long time. And while I'm happy to say that these kinds of depictions have fallen out of favor in more recent years, they haven't really been replaced with more positive representation, or any representation of note at all. There's more transgender representation certainly (*Transparent*, *The Danish Girl*, *Orange is the New Black*, etc.) but non-trans dressers have vanished. And since the last time they were seen was in these kinds of low-brow comedies, that means those films are still the closest thing to a pop culture touchstone that dressers have. And that just sucks.

As a result, when cross dressers try to come out to important people in their lives it becomes as much about explaining what this isn't as what it is. We're forced to try and explain our dressing in a feminine manner while at the same time trying to get the person we're telling to understand that it's not about sex and it's not about transitioning to a full-time woman. Of course, for some of us one or both of those is the case, and I don't mean to imply that makes it any easier for people in those situations. Ultimately, I can only really speak of my own experience and what's been shared with me by others. Many of us have a difficult time defining ourselves in our own minds because the only images of cross dressers we have to latch onto are either gay men or transitioning transsexuals. That can cause us to try to force ourselves to fit into one of these molds even if it isn't where we belong. It's reassuring to be able to point to something that's well-known and say, "That's me." When you're unable to do that it's unsettling, isolating, and potentially damaging.

I strongly suspect that this failure to fit the common templates was a large part of my own early floundering with my sexual orientation and the issue of whether or not I would ever want to transition to living as a woman full-time. The rationale was that if I'm a man who enjoys feeling like a woman part of the time then I must be transgender, or at the very least I must be bisexual. (This latter one is the more bizarre thought process for me to look back at now, knowing that gender identity and sexual preference are two completely different issues.) It would take time and a few close friends I could talk all this through with in order to realize that I didn't *have* to fit the available templates that I was seeing. If it doesn't feel right, then it's not for me, and it's not the end of the world to be outside of the box. Though, admittedly, it can be lonely at times if you can't find others like yourself. That is something I have done as time has passed which brings me no small amount of comfort.

CHAPTER ELEVEN

THE CONFIDENCE GAME

If there's one thing that looks good on anybody it's confidence. It's also your greatest shield against, well, pretty much anything. A healthy dose of confidence is going to ward off a surprising amount of hostility, because bullies like easy targets and someone who looks unsure of themselves is easy prey. Of course, exuding a sense of confidence when you're a man strolling down the street in a dress and heels you're half expecting to kill yourself in isn't the easiest thing in the world.

This is one of those cases where "fake it until you make it" really is the key phrase. What's so hard for many dressers is that we can't act confident because we don't feel confident. That lack of self-assurance is something people will notice, and we feel them noticing it, which reinforces the doubts and everything just spirals downwards. But it can just as easily work in the opposite direction.

This is something that a background in performance really helped me with. If you've ever been in a play or another form of live performance then odds are you've either screwed something up or been on stage when somebody else did. Somebody flubbed a line, or missed a cue, or the wrong sound effect was played by the folks in the booth, or whatever. But a good director will have instilled a very important lesson in you: you may *know* that something went wrong, but the audience won't know that unless you *act* like something went wrong. If you can keep in character and act like this was supposed to happen then the audience will have no idea that a mistake ever occurred.

Applying this to dressing meant that when I started to go out, I knew that I had to act like there was absolutely nothing wrong with what I was doing. Do people still notice that I'm a guy wearing women's clothes? I'm sure most of them do; I'm not 100% passable and I never will be. Do some people have a problem with what I'm doing? I have no doubt that this is the case. But to date I've never been publically confronted in over 10 years of dressing. Part of that is being careful about where I am at any given time, but I also chalk up a large degree to the fact that I don't act like I'm scared of what everybody is thinking. Of course, in the early days especially, I *was* scared of what they were thinking. But I didn't let it show. And the more I did this, the more I found that over time the confidence that I was faking was becoming genuine. Confidence became a self-fulfilling prophecy. It also made me more of an optimist. I managed to switch the mentality in my head. Initially, like most people, if I caught somebody watching me I would assume the worst. I would assume that they were judging me and disapproved of what I was doing. Now I'm able to take the optimistic view and think to myself, "They see how damn good I look." And if that's not what they're really thinking, that's their issue and not mine.

STRIVING TO BE PASSABLE

I mentioned earlier about my general attitude towards being "passable" as a woman when I'm doing the full look, but I want to address it more directly here. The idea of being passable is one that many of us can get hung up on. For a high percentage of us it's the ultimate goal: to be able to walk down the street with no one questioning our femininity and believing us to be naturally and completely female. There's certainly nothing wrong with having this as a goal. Most of us, however, need to accept that it's one that we will likely never attain.

The simple fact is that without the assistance of cosmetic surgery, hormone replacement therapy, or other physical interventions most of us will never be 100% passable as women (and, if we're being completely honest, even some people who undergo all those things still aren't). There are a countless number of "tells" that can and will give away a dresser. Some, like visible stubble or any noticeable body hair, can be address and rectified with a little work. Others can't be changed as readily, or even at all in many cases. I'm talking about things like muscular arms, square jaws, a prominent Adam's apples, height that is well above the average for a woman, broad shoulders, large hands or feet, and similar traits.

The thing to try and remember is that as long as we don't personally draw attention to these things, most people just walking by us on the street won't notice them. Your best defense against not being 100% passable is acting as though you are. Some might consider it "fake it until you make it," but however you think of it, the right attitude will do far more to carry you through being dressed in public than anything you do to hide or transform your body. To reiterate what I said before about confidence: you could be a stunningly convincing woman but if you look like you're uncomfortable in your own skin or that you're doing something wrong people will notice. They will then take a closer look and may spot a "tell" that will give you away. But if you act like there's no problem and exude confidence, most people won't take that closer look and any tells you may have won't be observed even though they're still there.

Part of the harm of the concept of being "passable" is that it implies passing for female as being an "all or nothing" proposition. You either pass for female or you don't. But it's not that simple. Many of us can pass for female at a distance, at a glance, or from the right angle. But almost all of us, no matter how feminine, can be spotted upon close inspection. For this reason, I've always hated this question: "Are you passable?" This was a common question back when I was in the chat rooms, and I never knew how to answer it. I knew the things that gave me away. I saw them immediately when I looked at myself. Therefore, I never was able to comfortably think of myself as passable. I've learned over time, however, that most people don't spot those giveaways unless they're looking intently for them, and most people just aren't paying me that much mind.

Rather than get hung up on the idea of passable, I prefer to focus on whether or not I look good. Because even when I was still figuring out makeup and knew I couldn't hope to pass I still felt that I looked good. At this point when I go out, even in full female presentation, I tend to assume that people are able to spot the fact that I'm not a woman by birth. This takes away the fear of "what if they know?" I assume that they know, and rather than focusing on whether or not I'm fooling anybody I focus my efforts on feeling attractive and feminine. A dresser does not need to be fooling the public at large to be beautiful. So when I walk down the street my mindset is: "They know I'm a man in a dress, but they also know that I look damn good in it." It's a form of body positivity. Much in the way that someone who is heavier than the current perceived ideal can either try to hide that or they can just wear whatever makes them feel good regardless of their size.

It took some time to arrive at that mindset. The desire to be passable was part of what fueled my earlier questions about my gender identity. I knew that the only way I'd ever be close to 100% passable would be through hormones, surgery, or both. When I thought more carefully about what I wanted for my life I realized that this was not the path I wanted to take. But I'd hung so much hope on the idea of being passable that it was difficult, for a time, to let these options go. It was only after I came to accept that being passable is not the only measure of cross dressing success that I was able to arrive at a healthier state of mind. In fact, I would say being passable isn't *any* measure of cross dressing success. You succeed at it if you feel right when you do it. Regardless of your reasons or the extent to which you take it or how you actually look when you do it, if it feels right then you're doing it right.

QUESTIONING GENDER IDENTITY

One of the things that I struggled with early on in my dressing was whether it was an end unto itself or whether it was just a first step in some sort of bigger gender transition. I touched on this in general a few times already but let's really dig into that. I found myself wondering if I am, in fact, transgender and if I should be taking steps to live full-time as a woman. It's a question that I've mostly settled for myself (at least as far as the issue of fully transitioning goes), but I am asked fairly frequently by other dressers and the public in general. Though I did ultimately come to the conclusion that I do not want to live full-time as a woman, your own conclusion may be different. But in any case, I think it may help some people to lay out the dilemma and how I came to the conclusion that I did.

There were two major reasons why this was even a question in my mind. The first was just the lack of a point of reference for being a part-time dresser, which I've brought up a few times already. Back when I started dressing regularly my understanding of what it meant to be a dresser was either a gay man or a person who wanted to be a woman full-time. I just had no frame of reference for cross dressing to mean anything else. It's reflective of how our experiences often limit our perceptions. Until we see some kind of outside confirmation that living a certain way is possible, it's not always easy to imagine it from scratch. Nobody likes to be alone, and not seeing part-time dressers in my early days made me think something like that would leave me without a community.

The other thing that made me question my gender identity was how much enjoyment I got out of dressing. It was exciting and thrilling and fulfilling in a way that's still hard to put into words. For a time, I found myself wondering if that meant I should be doing it more, so that I could experience that rush all the time. Initially, I failed to recognize that part of the reason it was energizing had something to do with the fact that it was a special thing I did from time to time rather than something I was trying to keep up constantly. I would later learn (when I was doing more frequent shows in NYC) that for me, dressing can be as exhausting as it is fulfilling. Doing it for longer stretches or with little to no downtime in between often ended up leaving me much more drained than I would have thought previously, a realization which served to ground me a bit.

Ultimately, the way I came to realize that I did not, in fact, want to live my life full-time as a woman was by examining my day-to-day existence as a man. While it's true that I always looked forward to dressing and being Vera, I didn't feel that my life was empty or somehow out of whack when I wasn't doing it. I think the hallmark of being transgender, at least from my observations, is gender-dysphoria—a deep-seated feeling of being wrong in the skin you were born in. You go about your day as the sex you were assigned at birth and something about it feels off. It feels like a burden, and maybe you don't even know why. As much as I love being Vera, I've never felt wrong day to day as a man. Being Vera is a wonderful thing but it's not a relief from some ever-present pain of having to be a man the rest of the time. And coming to this understanding of myself was what helped me start to find a better balance. I know that dressing will always be a part of my life but it's unlike to ever be the entirety of it. Of course, that's me, and each will come to their own conclusions with time and help. What's more, while this stance that I would not be happy living full-time as a woman has not changed, it is worth pointing out that things have shifted somewhat for me in more recent years into a less rigidly-defined and more fluid space.

STRADDLING THE GENDER LINE

As I said, I strongly believe that I will never transition to living as a woman full-time. The very idea makes me tired. And, to be blunt, there are times that I flat out love being a man. However, recently there has been a bit of a shift in how I've started operating on a day-to-day basis. For about a decade I basically treated dressing as Vera like a light switch: it was either on or it was off. Either I was done up in full dress, body shaved with makeup and a wig, or I was in complete boy mode. And for that 10-year timespan that suited me just fine. More recently, however, I've begun to experiment with the middle ground, treating my gender more like a dimmer switch: something that has many middle settings to adjust rather than being all one or the other.

I think there were many small things over time that led to this decision to explore a less clearly-defined approach to my gender, though I can point to one thing in particular that got me actively thinking about it. During my involvement with the Green Mountain Cabaret I developed a new stage persona. Green Mountain Cabaret is a burlesque group operating on the opposite side of the state from where I live.

I am friends with many of the members and a semi-frequent guest performer at their monthly shows. If it were feasible, I really would like to join the troupe proper, but the commuting time makes the required rehearsals impossible for me. However, I was able to get more involved by joining the ranks of the hosts, which comes with a time commitment that is workable for me.

The hosts of the Green Mountain Cabaret are the Peepers family—as of this writing it's comprised of Lief Peepers, Thom Peepers, Beaux Peepers, Prudie Peepers, Jeepers Peepers, and Marsha Mallow-Peepers. I auditioned for a hosting spot and got in, and was given the option of hosting as Vera or creating a new persona. The latter made more sense, if only because one of the great things about Vera as a performance persona is that she's very malleable. I can do geeky numbers, angry numbers, sexy numbers, or anything else I can think of. For hosting, I was going to need to lock down a more consistent persona and I preferred to do that with something new rather than try to shackle and limit Vera's onstage possibilities. Thus was born Snow Peepers: because there's no Peepers like Snow Peepers, like no Peepers we know.

The concept behind Snow is what I refer to as "genderfuck" (a term I picked up from my friend Syd London during my time in New York). How *I* practice it makes it kind of the opposite of androgyny. As I mentioned when we talked about labels, androgyny is generally not having clear sexual characteristics or gender markers of either of the two standard sexes. Genderfuck is outwardly, visibly, and deliberately displaying the characteristics of multiple genders at the same time.

Confusion is the new sexy.

Snow is a fun character and one I've enjoyed developing. I don't wear a wig as Snow which, as I mentioned, was historically the one item that makes me feel the most feminine. I also use a packer (something usually reserved for drag kings or female-to-male cross dressers) to create a frankly obscene bulge in the crotch area. And I also tend to make use of my largest breast forms on top of that. So creating this deliberately-blended stage persona started getting my mind into a headspace where I was ready to start experimenting with blurring the gender line in my daily life more than I had.

The first thing I did in trying out this middle ground was to get my ears pierced. I'd opted for clip on earrings up to that point because I never really cared for the pierced ear look on men (it tends to read "pirate" to me). But in starting to think of my day-to-day life as being less definitively male, the idea of having earrings became much more appealing. Obviously it opens me up for so many possibilities as Vera as well, and I found a nice selection of studs and smaller hoops that I'm comfortable with for day-to-day wear at my job.

This middle ground has also put possibly getting tattoos back onto the table for me. For a long time I had planned to get a tattoo, and had even worked out exactly what it would be and where it would go. However, I kept chickening out when it came down to actually scheduling the work to be done. I came to realize that part of what was holding me back was that, in general, I love the look of tattoos on women, but tend to be neutral at best when it comes to tattoos on men. This means that, mentally, it got filed away along with earrings as something I might regret since I live most of life in male mode. But as I've started to see myself as not definitively one or the other, the possibility of finally getting my tattoos has crept back into my head. I don't know if I'll actually pull the trigger on this (I haven't as of this writing) but my mind has opened up to it whereas before I thought the issue was more or less closed.

Now, to say that my day-to-day life is becoming less defined doesn't mean that I no longer have a male mode at all. At work I still keep things pretty strictly masculine. There's a part of me that would love to be able to have nail polish on a daily basis, but when it comes to my job that's just not the best idea. Sure, there's nothing in the code of conduct or dress code that says I *couldn't* wear nail polish. However, I know it could possibly elicit some odd reactions or even discomfort from other employees and I'd just as soon not have to deal with that. Multiple people in my life have worked in Human Resources, so I've heard enough about the behind-the-scenes workings of companies to know that if an employee is throwing off the vibe of the workplace (even if it's by doing something that isn't strictly forbidden) then they run the risk of being looked at more closely for a legitimate reason to be let go. From an employer's perspective it's more trouble to keep an employee that makes everybody else feel weird than it is to find to a legally-acceptable reason to dismiss them. It's not fair, to be sure, but it's also the reality. The earrings I get away with because enough other male employees have earrings that it doesn't raise any eyebrows. However, I know better than to push my luck too far.

The main point I'm getting at with all of this is that, even after all these years, my journey isn't really over. I'm still evolving. And that's ok. My exploration of living a more gender-fluid life day to day doesn't mean that I was somehow wrong in living the more binary life of either all man or all woman that I was doing before. It just means that what feels right has shifted and I am choosing to shift along with it.

CHAPTER TWELVE

CROSS DRESSING AND SEXUAL ORIENTATION

Perhaps the single most confusing thing about cross dressing, for both those who do it and those who try to understand it (spouses, family, etc.) is how it relates to sexual orientation. If you are a man dressing as a woman, does that make you gay? If you still like women does that make you a lesbian in a man's body? Are you automatically considered a bisexual at least? All of these questions swirl around the heads of dressers, especially in their early days of exploring their femininity, so let me make this as clear as I can: your gender identity and how you choose to dress have *nothing* to do with your sexual orientation.

The major issue around all of this is how narrow the frame of reference is for non-transitioning dressers. As I talked about earlier, there really is very little in the popular culture for a cross dresser with no plans to transition into life as a woman to grab onto for reference. In films and TV, men dressing as women are either doing so for the purposes of comedy or as some expression of homosexuality (i.e. drag queens in pride parades). Simply put, there are almost no straight cross dressers actively out there for people to use as a point of reference. As mentioned, Eddie Izzard is the notable exception, and he even addresses this topic in some of his stand-up material. However, he hasn't been dressing outside of his stage shows for some time now, so people can view it as something he just does in his comedy routines. As a rule, if a straight or non-transitioning man is shown to be dressing as a woman in a TV show or in a film it's almost never truly by choice. Rather, it's something forced on them by unfortunate circumstances and generally played for laughs (as in some of the painful films I mentioned earlier or even the classic *Some Like It Hot*). As a result of not having a common frame of reference, once a dresser identifies the need in themselves to dress as a woman it almost instantly stirs up questions about their own sexuality.

For quite some time during my early days I wondered if I was gay. Looking back on it now this seems like a silly notion, but that's the benefit of hindsight. Part of the reason I like to appear as a woman is because they are what I'm attracted to. It's a bit of a narcissistic thing in my case, I'll admit, but I want to look in the mirror and see a person that I myself would want to be with sexually. But because dressing as a woman was so closely tied to gay men in my mind, I thought at the very least I *must* be bisexual. This led to a certain amount of experimentation, the majority of which never really felt quite right. Yet despite the fact that it wasn't working for me, I kept pushing the issue and tried to force myself to fit this mold of what I thought a dresser was supposed to be. It probably only confused the issue further that in those early days I tended to flirt online with men and even enjoyed it. But looking back, I know that was out of a need for attention rather than an actual inherent attraction to men. In the end I'm attracted to the feminine form and female attributes, and how I choose to dress doesn't change that.

What I wish I'd done is just taken my dressing out of the equation altogether. What clothes you put on or how you choose to present yourself in terms of gender has zero to do with what you find attractive. And it's your attractions, and your attractions alone, that are what determine your sexual preference. As a society we're very fixated on labels, on finding out exactly what we are and assigning a name to it. When you start messing with gender definitions it muddles everything. I've seen terms like "trans-lesbian" referring to male-to-female transgendered people who are attracted to women, or "transbian" used for transgendered persons who are attracted to other transgender folk. Speaking personally, these sorts of overly-defined terms just make my head spin.

Forget the labels, forget even what gender you currently are or want to be. When it comes to trying to figure out your sexual preference you need to strip all of that away and ask yourself only one question: what are you attracted to? Don't answer that question with, "Well, I'm a cross dresser who prefers..." It doesn't matter what you are. Your sexual preference is dependent on only one thing: what you are sexually attracted to. How you yourself identity in terms of your own gender doesn't enter into this equation. If you are attracted to women that won't change, even if you alter your gender through surgery. We think labels are clarifying, but in this realm they are confusing. So when somebody asks, "Are you gay?" or any such equivalent, just answer, "I'm attracted to ___" and let them figure out the label themselves. It doesn't have to be your problem. If you want a simple phrase to keep in your back pocket, use this one: "Gender identity is who you are. Sexual orientation is who you are attracted to. They're not the same thing."

SEXY DOES NOT MEAN SEXUAL

One of the things that can be the most difficult for non-dressers to understand is that a dresser's desire to look sexy does not mean that dressing is itself a sexual act. Don't get me wrong, for many dressers it is an inherently sexual act and a part of their sexual expression. And that's fine. However, if dressing is only partly about sex for you, or indeed isn't about sex at all, then it's a bit tricky for others to fully understand and it can be confusing for us as well.

I know that in my early days, along with some questions about my true gender and sexual preference, there was some confusion as to whether or not dressing was part of my sex life or not. It never really entered into the bedroom for me, but I couldn't deny the thrill I would get when I looked at myself in the mirror and was really happy with and even attracted to what I saw. It was a feeling that, at times, I mistook for sexual excitement, when it fact it was just the thrill of being sexy.

I don't know if it's the case for all dressers, but I know that for me I rarely feel sexy as a man. I can think that I look good, but I've never really wrapped my head around what I can do to make myself sexy in a masculine way. I don't fit the generic "sexy man" types: I'm not particularly muscled, I don't work out or play sports, I can't grow decent-looking facial hair, and I'm not in a rock band. As a result, I'm usually pleasantly shocked when somebody gives me a genuine compliment on my appearance when I'm presenting as a man. It's not that I think I look lousy. I think I look good but I don't equate my masculine appearance with being attractive.

This led to some confusion when I would get dressed up as a woman and feel flat out sexy. I couldn't understand what I was feeling. It was this kind of thrill in the pit of my stomach and a slight flutter in my heart. For a time I assumed this was some sort of sexual excitement, even though I wasn't becoming physically aroused. It was just the only thing I could connect this feeling to that made any sense. As time went on, and I got a firmer sense of my own sexuality and preferences, I came to realize that something feeling sexy is not the same as that thing being sexual.

This can be a very confusing area for many of us, especially since for many the line between sexy and sexual is pretty blurred. I mean, if there's any sexual component to our dressing at all then that will be amplified when we dress in a way that makes us feel sexy. But that still doesn't mean that dressing is or has to be a sexual end. I honestly believe that part of the reason I see so many overly-sexualized personas among dressers is that they can't separate the feeling of being sexy from being outwardly sexual. It all becomes one thing, when a bit of distinction would do most of us some good, I think.

Feeling sexy is really just about you and how you feel. Being sexual involves other people in some way. That's not always easy for us to understand, and it's even more difficult for others to understand. I'm talking largely of the men who find dressers sexually attractive here. When I'm out I'll give everybody a pass the first time they come on to me, because they're just taking a shot in the dark. I'll politely indicate that I'm not interested so that they can move along, or at least change modes to just being friendly. However, a disturbing number of men will continue to pester, and this male aggression isn't always easy to deal with. Men like this are the same kind who assume a woman in a short skirt and high heels is just asking to be treated like a sex object and get cat-called. It's the breed of man who used to claim that rape victims had it coming based on how they were dressed. They may know enough to not make that claim anymore, but the mentality is still deeply imbedded. It's objectification, pure and simple, and it reinforces this idea that we can't be sexy without also being sexual.

You need to give yourself permission to feel sexy without feeling some sort of obligation to also express yourself in a sexual fashion because of it. You are in control of your sexuality; it's not determined by the kinds of clothes you choose to wear on any given day. You're allowed to go out in an outfit that makes you feel sexy and beautiful with no sexual intentions whatsoever. A short skirt does not make you a sex toy. It doesn't even make you a tease. This is a term thrown out by rejected men who can't handle the idea that a woman (cisgender, transgender, or cross dresser) can dress how she likes for herself. It's not about impressing them. Dressing a certain way doesn't make you a tease, or a toy, or a slut. You are your own woman, however you choose to be. It is your choice alone whether you wish to be sexual. It is not determined by your attire and some horny jerk's assumptions.

THE BATHROOM DILEMMA

For dressers going out and about in public there are all sorts of "issues", many of which are ultimately in our own heads. Unless you're living in an overtly intolerant area, most problems with going out in women's clothes are just your own fears. Even when there is a legitimate basis for these fears we tend to blow them out of proportion. The idea that we will be spotted as men is a big one that many of us have to get over. The idea that anybody who does spot us as men even cares is a more important idea to get rid of. There is, however, one issue that is very real and worth talking about: which bathroom do we use?

Do I look like I belong here? Photo by Syd London.

This is a big enough issue that I feel very strongly it's something you need to have a plan for *before* you actually go out in public. If you're going out for an extended period (or going out and planning to drink anything, even water) you will want to do a little research ahead of time about the places you plan to go to. There are basically a few different situations you may find yourself in, and each will have a slightly different way that you'll need to handle it. I know that various states have been pushing for legislation that actually makes it a crime for even a post-op trans person to use any bathroom other than the one designated for the sex on their birth certificate. Some municipalities are going the other way and requiring local businesses to have non-gender specific bathrooms. It's a landscape that is in fairly constant flux as laws are proposed and then challenged, so I can't really address the bathroom question directly in terms of legality for a given area. Do a bit of research in your area to see what ordinances (if any) are in place and act accordingly with the law as best as you're able to in order to avoid a sticky situation. That said, here are some general rules of thumb to be applied in places where there aren't any actual laws in place to dictate where you pee.

First, let me say that if you're going to a trans-themed event, or to a bar or club that is known to be trans friendly, then you should be safe to go ahead and use the lady's room. In those sorts of situations that's the expectation. At any sort of pride, trans, or drag event, dressers and transgendered persons are expected to use the bathroom of the gender they are currently presenting as, regardless of what they may be underneath the clothes. So for those going out mostly to trans nights at gay bars or other events that cater to dressers, there really isn't anything to worry about. Pop on into the lady's room and don't stress over it.

However, if you're going to a place that isn't specifically catering to trans folk then things can get a little bit trickier. Honestly, I'd advise you to avoid using the bathroom at all if you can help it. I say this largely based on what I myself am: I am a cross dresser. Sometimes I present as a woman, sometimes as a man, and sometimes I present in a way that isn't clearly either male or female. I'm not planning to transition to living full-time as a woman. In other words, if I'm being blunt about it, I am the thing that the fear mongers say people should all be terrified of: a man who feels like a woman that day and as a result goes into the ladies' room. Frankly, I don't need to be lending any credence to people who use this image to try and oppress members of the trans community, and I actually consider avoiding bathrooms as doing my part to help.

But sometimes you simply need a bathroom. Maybe it's the obvious reason, maybe you need to adjust your tuck, whatever. Should you absolutely need to use a bathroom, the next question, after the general nature of the location, is the bathroom itself, specifically if it's meant for one or multiple occupants. If it's a single occupant bathroom, the kind where you would go inside, lock the door behind you, and be the only one in there, then you can feel free to use either one. In this case I would favor the lady's room again. It's true you may get an odd look or two coming out from those waiting for it after you, but I think it's still the better option than to be coming out of the men's room in a dress (again, local laws notwithstanding).

Things get difficult in situations where the bathroom is a row of stalls and there may be other people already in there or they can enter in behind you. This really is a bit of a no-win situation, and in all honesty, I would avoid even entering these types of bathrooms if it's not at a trans-friendly location or event. There are problems with these sorts of set ups regardless of whether you go into the ladies' room or the men's. If you were to enter the ladies' room there are potential legal issues, as mentioned before. Depending on the laws of your area, if any of the women inside are uncomfortable with you being there the police can end up being involved, even if there aren't specific laws in place banning your presence.

On the flipside, going into a men's room in dress can be flat out dangerous. While women may not like you in their bathroom, and may even make a fuss, it's very rare that they would ever attempt to physically confront you. Men, on the other hand, are a different breed. Entering the men's room in dress runs the risk of encountering men who simply can't handle what it is you're doing. Whether it's transphobia or homophobia, there are men out there who want to hurt us. In a public place we have the safety of other eyes and those who might hurt us are generally kept in check by that fact. However, a bathroom is more private. It's still technically a public place, but it's just private enough that these kinds of men feel that they can get away with hurting people like us. This is compounded by the fact that it's not uncommon for even stall-type bathrooms to be lockable from the inside, trapping us with people who mean us harm. I'm sorry if this all sounds rather alarmist, but it's a very real danger and one that should be avoided.

Things are getting better. Very recently in my home state of Vermont a law was passed dictating that all single occupancy bathrooms have to be marked for use by anyone. If a building's bathrooms are occupied by only one person then they can no longer be arbitrarily designated as "Men" and "Women". I'm not sure if Vermont is the first start to have made this particular move or not, but it is at least among the first. And hopefully the first of many.

So to review: know what laws are on the books in your area. Honestly, it may be best to avoid using public bathrooms at all if not at a trans- or pride-related event or location. A single occupant bathroom, where you are not sharing the space with other people, is acceptable. The thing to avoid is multiple stalls. It's best to avoid this situation completely, but if you absolutely have to go and can't wait or find a safer locale, then opt for the ladies' room every time and avoid men's rooms. At the end of the day you're better off explaining yourself to an authority figure than risking assault.

CROSS DRESSING WHILE STRAIGHT IN AN LGBTQ+ WORLD

For people like me who identify as more or less straight (i.e. physiologically male and overwhelmingly attracted to females or vice versa) and cross dress, there's the surprisingly difficult to answer question of where we belong. I've talked about some of the communities that I've been part of (burlesque, drag, etc.) but it's been a matter of finding individuals within those communities who embraced me. In general terms, a straight dresser doesn't really belong anywhere. One would assume that we're part of the grand LGBTQ+ rainbow, and I suppose that we are, but our placement there can be... contentious.

I'm going to apologize in advance for some of the generalizations that are about to follow. I do consider myself to be part of the LBGQ+ community, and feel increasingly embraced by it. However, I'd be remiss and disingenuous if I didn't talk about the fact that there are some within this same community who have a very strong distaste for what I do, how I live, and others like me. I don't intend this to be a finger-wagging or shaming of the community that I love. But in the end, I can only speak to my experience. And in that experience, I've gotten harsher pushback and hatred from members of the LGBTQ+ community than I have from conservative reactionaries (the people one would assume would be the haters).

I've touched on the fact that gay men tend to have very mixed reactions to crossdressers in general. However, that reaction is more likely to be a sour one if you're a dresser who is not attracted to men. In their eyes there's just no connection between you and them. I've gotten a very chilly reception for having the nerve to step into a gay bar on any night other than a specifically-designated drag night, and I've been told by other dressers of the same experience. They're not wrong in their belief that I don't really belong there. But that vibe is sometimes brought across in an overly harsh manner, especially since many dressers are turning up due to a lack of anywhere else to go.

Funnily enough, lesbians have been among the most inherently receptive of me as a cross dresser. I'm honestly not sure why this is. But it's been the case consistently for as long as I've been going out in public. I'm not sure how many other dressers experience this, since I suspect my ties to the drag king community put me in more lesbian spaces than is typical for a cross dresser. But I've always been welcomed in those spaces, to a degree that still surprises me. I suppose it could be that since I'm presenting female and am attracted to women it sets me as something similar to a lesbian. At least, I'm close to that than a gay man.

I don't have much to say on the subject of bisexuals. There isn't really an organized "bisexual community" the way there is with lesbian, gay, or transgender. And I also know that bisexuals have had their own problems of acceptance within the community. A surprising number of people still insist that bisexuality is not even a real thing. Since bisexuals are not as unified as other parts of the LGBTQ+ community, I can't really make any generalizations about this group.

Ultimately, the harshest pushback comes from the part of the LGBTQ+ community many assume cross dressers fall under: transgender. To be blunt about it, the most hostile people I've ever had to deal with have been transwomen (i.e. assigned male at birth and have transitioned or are working towards transitioning to life as a female). It's not the majority, but those who get upset with me get *really* upset. It's not all that hard to figure out why when you think about it. Some transwomen have what I can only describe as a violent gag reflex at the thought that my existence means people will lump them together with somebody who's "just a man in a dress." Transwomen obviously go through a great deal of crap in order to live as the women that they are. I understand not wanting to be viewed in the same light as someone who's able and willing to just take all of this stuff off and be a man again. The assumption that cross dressing is some kind of sexual kink also rears its head again here. It's understandable that transwomen wouldn't want the lives they live every day lumped together with somebody else's fetish, especially given how often they are already fetishized by certain men. But the open hostility I've encountered doesn't help anyone. I've been told flat out, "You're not even trans, so stop acting like a woman!" Apparently in some people's minds there's a minimum requirement to be allowed to act feminine, and if you don't meet it then you're mocking or damaging them.

I wrote an article in 2015 that went up on Cracked.com (and in a way served a proof of concept for this book) titled "7 Things You Learn as a Straight Guy Who Cross Dresses." While there were a few nasty comments of the "fucking faggot" variety, it was my pointing out that cross dressers aren't universally welcome in the LGBTQ+ community that resulted in the most heated diatribes in the comment section. Depressingly, a vocal minority of commenters identifying as trans ended up proving the point by going on lengthy rants about how cross dressers damage their image and how our very existence hurts their community.

I get the anger. Many transwomen have had to work extremely hard to distance themselves from casual or sexual cross dressers in the eyes of the public. But that association isn't the fault of cross dressers. We don't dress with any agenda to damage or undermine anyone. It's the public at large that needs to be educated on the difference. This is something that is going to be a slow slog to get through, but I'd like to think that transwomen and cross dressers can work together on it rather than taking up opposite sides when there's no need to be fighting in the first place.

Which brings us to the part of LGBTQ+ that actually fits me best: Queer. In my time being out, the concept of queer as part of the community has grown greatly. In my earlier days, the community was mostly still just going with LGBT and didn't have the Q at all. Since its placement is a more recent development, I'll explain for anybody who's confused. Where in the past "queer" was just another term for "gay," it has more recently become something of a catch-all for non-straight and non-gender conforming folks who don't cleanly fit the other four letters. This is where you'll find people who are asexual, agender, genderfluid, and non-binary among many other things. A bit like bisexuals, this isn't as much of a formalized community as lesbian, gay, or transgender. But in this case I think that has more to do with its relative newness. Not that queer people are new, but recognition that there's a whole bunch of us who are clearly outside of the heterosexual and cisgender paradigm without being lesbian, gay, bisexual, or transgender is pretty recent. As queer has become better understood and more embraced by the LGBTQ+ community (and even some outside of it), I've been seeing the pushback happen less often and with less anger. So perhaps finally things are getting a bit better on that front.

CHAPTER THIRTEEN

COMING OUT: WHEN, HOW, AND TO WHOM

I want to come back to two questions I frequently get asked: "When do I come out and how do I do it?" Except to ask those questions skips over the one that needs to come first: "*Should* I come out at all?" I hate advising anybody to stay in the closet, but I've found myself having to do it on more than a few occasions because it was the lesser evil of all available options.

The main situation where I've advised people to not come out has to do with young dressers, usually still in high school, who feel very strongly or know based on experience that their parents will not accept them. I can't even begin to understand how this feels, because it's something I've never had to deal with. I may have had reservations about telling my mother but it was never out of a fear of rejection. However, the first thing to realize is that you can't force someone to understand. I know that the young people asking me this are praying for some magic phrase or technique that will make their families accept them, but these things simply don't exist. If you truly believe that your family will reject you and possibly expel you from the house or try to force you to change then it may be best to keep it hidden from them.

Of course, if we're close to our families at all, even if we know they won't accept our dressing, keeping something this big is going to weigh on us over time. So I don't advise keeping it hidden indefinitely. What I recommend in these cases is to either wait until you have moved out of the house, or failing that, know for certain there is a safe place you can go if you are thrown out. (This could be with a friend, a relative, or at a local support group.) I feel it's best not to be under the direct power of a parent who is liable to reject you before telling them about your dressing.

For those who are ready, or who don't have families likely to outright reject them, that doesn't really make it any easier. I feel strongly that the clichéd scene of an LGBTQ+ person sitting their whole family down to announce these things is ill-advised. It makes it easier for the person coming out, because you only have to do it once, but honestly it's not the best for your family to just have it dumped on them like that. What I recommend is starting one-on-one with the family member you're most comfortable with and who is most likely to support you. This could be one of your parents, a sibling, an aunt or uncle, or even a cousin. But get somebody on your side first (and who can possibly be in the room with you) before you start tackling the family members who may have a harder time with your dressing. Even then I recommend taking family members in as small a grouping as you can, if not one at a time. It's a longer process this way, but I think it minimizes the chance for a big scene.

The situation for young dressers is fairly unique and it doesn't necessarily apply to adults who don't have to worry about being thrown out of the house. Of course, even adults can still face rejection from those in their lives. The big question here is who you should be coming out to. I feel this is largely dependent on what cross dressing is to you. For example, if dressing for you is primarily a sexual act, something you do for sexual gratification, then really the only person who truly needs to know is your sexual partner. I mean, you wouldn't tell your parents or siblings that you were into leather and bondage or dominance play pornography would you? Of course not. It's none of their business and they wouldn't want to know anyway. So if it's a bedroom practice it should be kept on the same privacy level as any other sexual practice: the only people who need to know are the ones you're inviting into your bed. If it's a bigger part of your day-to-day life then it may be necessary to come out to more family and friends, but the extent of that can vary.

For adults, the big fear is always coming out to significant others. For those in a newer relationship the big question is always "when should I tell them?" This is a delicate question. I should first establish that I do *not* believe it is ever wise to try to hide this from a significant other. If you start to date someone and keep this from them, when they find out (and they will eventually) there's going to be a bigger problem than your dressing: the betrayal of trust. For you to hide something this big about yourself fundamentally undermines the openness and trust that a relationship needs to be built on. Whether or not they accept the dressing almost becomes irrelevant, because through your actions you've basically said, "In all these years I never trusted you enough to tell you this."

So it has to be shared, but when? In my mind this is a third date conversation. When I say that I don't mean you must wait until the third date specifically like it's a clear line in the sand. Rather, I'm basing this on the general progression of dates in a new relationship that is going well. On the first date it's all the surface stuff: what you do for a living, what movies you like, your favorite color, etc. Second dates will usually start to dig a little deeper: family history, dating history, plans for the future. Third dates are when people tend to tackle the more touchy things that could be deal breakers: religion, politics, and whether or not they want children. I feel that cross dressing is a third date conversation because most of us don't want to just go around telling everybody in the first few minutes "I wear dresses." Also, if you announce this too soon you risk that being how the other person defines you. You want to give them a chance to get to know you as a more complete person first. At the same time, you don't want to wait much longer than this, because you risk crossing the line into trust-betrayal by hiding it.

How you should actually go about telling someone you think you might want to build a life with is a question that nobody can answer but you. I know that sounds like a cop out, but it's true. Just like with teenagers telling their parents, there is no magic phrase that will make it go down smoother. Just be plain, straight forward, and open to questions, because odds are there will be quite a few.

Of course, the folks who have it the toughest of all are those who either discovered late in life that dressing fills a need for them or who tried to hide and suppress it for so long they're now in a long-term relationship or marriage with someone who doesn't know about this side of them. In many ways these are no-win situations: there will be damage to the relationship, it's just a question of extent. The lucky ones have a significant other who, though likely hurt, understands the fear that kept the person from revealing this until now.

Sadly, those tend to be the exception. This is a major contributor to cases of married adult men coming out and starting to transition very late in life, usually after their children have moved out of the house. They wait because they know it will effectively end their marriages.

As frightening, and even potentially damaging, as it is I've seen the cycle that closeted dressers who don't come out get trapped in. It quickly becomes a cycle of guilt and purging. It must be remembered that we dress because it fills a need for us, and though the nature of that need can vary from dresser to dresser it is there for all of us. And it's a need that is very difficult to ignore, meaning most who are closeted are doing some degree of dressing in secret. In trying to hide it we link a sense of guilt to what we are doing. As a result, closeted dressers tend to hit a breaking point of guilt where they say, "No more, I'm stopping," and they dispose of their feminine items and swear off it forever. Or at least they try to. Because that root need doesn't go away just because you threw the clothes out. And it starts again, maybe with a pair of panties or a tube of lipstick, until it hits the breaking point once more and the cycle starts over.

Purgers or not, those who hide dressing from significant others for a very long time make themselves vulnerable to creating and then having to hide an entire second life. I've seen more instances than I can count of married men getting dressed and sometimes seeking sexual encounters in an attempt to fulfill a need that they can't bring themselves to tell their wives. Some would not consider themselves gay, but the more they try to bury who they are, the more extreme the version of their feminine side is that emerges. Lies and secrets build up until they become something far bigger than the simple truth ever was. Honesty in this situation is never easy, but it is often the best option; I've yet to meet the married dresser who could go indefinitely without being caught.

ON THE JOB

While family, significant others, and close friends are the most pressing people for dresser to consider coming out to, there are other considerations as well. The other major thing to tackle is coming out at the job or not. Exactly where and how your work life fits into your dressing life will vary from dresser to dresser. Those actually moving towards a transition are going to have to cross this bridge sooner or later, while those who dress as a bedroom activity will want to keep it completely separate. For those who fall somewhere in the middle it's not easy to know if or to what extent to come out at work.

I'm sure some of you are wondering why coming out at work would even be a question in the first place? Why would anybody invite that kind of scrutiny when (as of the time of this writing) most states don't offer any kind of workplace protection in regards to gender identity or expression? It should be understood those who are "out" in some form at work didn't call a company meeting and give a PowerPoint presentation in high heels and a pencil skirt. Rather, it's usually something that happens gradually.

Most of us end up making friends with some of our coworkers, which can often be the gateway to some form of being out at work. As you make friends, and if those friendships become close, you may reach a point where you want to come out to that person. But then there are questions of discretion, and what kind of damage might happen if your coworkers who aren't close friends find out. There is no clear-cut answer to this dilemma, and it really is going to vary from workplace to workplace.

The first thing you should do is figure out what protections, if any, exist in your state for LGBTQ+ people in the workplace. Until LGBTQ+ becomes a protected class at the federal level the same as religion, sex, and disabilities, it's vital to know if you reside in a state with or without such protections. If your state doesn't have any in place then it is perfectly legal (though probably not a good PR move) for your employer to fire you due to your nontraditional gender identification. Even if you *do* live in a state that has some protections in place, that should not be taken as a license to start coming to work in pumps and a stylish blouse one day out of the blue. Even if you have protection, it's very difficult to prove discrimination and you're only protected if you can show that your gender identity was the primary reason you were fired. Your employer may find more "legitimate" reasons to remove you from the workplace that have nothing to do with your dressing (relating to performance issues, downsizing or layoffs, etc.) so always be aware of your own level of vulnerability. If the people at the head of your company aren't comfortable with any of this, it's not very difficult for them to find or orchestrate a legally-allowed reason to let you go.

Beyond worries about actually keeping your job, there's also the issue of general comfort level. Even if, for the moment, we totally set aside any concerns about being fired, your dressing could still cause tension or awkwardness between you and your coworkers. Some people do not and will never understand cross dressing, and some hold very negatively-biased opinions about those who do it. Now, I'm not saying you should run your life based on what a handful of people are liable to think. But you do need to have a realistic sense of how many of those kinds of people may be in your workplace. If it's just one or two people who you don't work with directly then that's very different from an environment where many of those you work close with may not accept you.

I've found that I've worked in what I consider almost the polar opposite. When I was working in NYC I became friends with a number of coworkers, including my immediate supervisor. The company had a very laid-back and fun-loving environment, and those in it were largely open-minded. Therefore, I didn't have a great deal of fear about revealing myself. I started with those I knew I could trust to keep it quiet so it wouldn't spread faster than I was ready for. After a while I didn't so much advertise it in general as simply not bother to hide it. I just kind of assumed that everybody knew, and those who might have had a distaste for it knew enough not to say anything. After a while I even put up advertisements for the burlesque show I produced and hosted as Vera on the company board (after seeking permission to do so from HR).

After moving to Vermont things took a rather drastic shift. After a bit of temping I landed in a company just across the border in New Hampshire. To say that the environment was different from what I'd gotten used to in NYC is an understatement. Living and working in a more rural environment meant that I was working with much more conservatively-minded people. I remember the first time I heard a person in a supervisor position use the term "queer" in a derogatory fashion. My heart stopped, but clearly nobody else in the room was bothered by it. I was actually the target of eye rolling from some coworkers when I said it made me a little uncomfortable. To be fair, she wasn't directly referring to a person as being "queer," she was using it to describe something that just didn't make sense to her. But just the fact that she could casually toss off the term in that way and nobody besides me so much as blinked told me everything I needed to know. It was an uncomfortable place to be because, despite being fairly out and open in most other areas of my life, I now felt more in the closet than I ever had before. It's not like I actually wanted to be out at work. I wasn't making the kinds of friends at this job that I'd share this part of my life with. But to have to go from not worrying about who knew to actively being sure I concealed it was disconcerting.

The funny thing is that I was eventually found out. I don't know by whom, but I know that for a time there were at least two people in the company aware of my dressing. One day I was called into the Human Resources office. This is much like being called into the principal's office at school; it could be no big deal but you always fear the worst. The head of HR started by asking me a question which I now know really shouldn't have been asked. She asked me if I was Vera Wylde. I confirmed that I was, which didn't seem to illicit much reaction from her one way or the other. She then said that it had been brought to her attention that as Vera I'd put up some Twitter posts during work hours. I was quick to point out that any posts that went up during the day would have been done on my lunch break, as my timecard and the timestamp on the tweets would easily confirm. She agreed, but asked that I not post during the day just to avoid making ripples. That was pretty much it.

As I said, I now know that she really shouldn't have asked me if I was Vera in the first place, especially since the concern wasn't strictly speaking about my dressing but rather my activities during work hours. It's not that there's anything against the law about her asking—there's no equivalent to "don't ask, don't tell" in the workplace—but it was simply a bad idea on her part. By acknowledging that she, and by extension the company, are aware that I cross dress it opened her up to liability. She'd have been much better off never letting on that she knew. You can't discriminate against what you don't know (or at least, what it can't be proven that you know).

Like most states, New Hampshire has "at will" employment, meaning they can let me go without cause if they feel like it. There are certain reasons that they aren't allowed to fire me, but I'd have to prove that I was fired for those specific reasons (being disabled or of a certain religion, for example). Also, at the time of my hiring and until very recently New Hampshire had no protection for one's gender identity or gender expression. However, there *was* protection for sexual orientation (i.e. they can't fire me for being gay, or for *believing* that I'm gay). Given the strong association that most people make between cross dressing and being gay, this means it's fairly easy for me to infer that, of whatever pool of people in the company know of my dressing, some of them assume I'm also gay. This opens the company up to potential issues and gives me a miniscule degree of protection that I wouldn't have otherwise. However, it doesn't really change the fact that there are people who know about this side of my life and I have no idea who they are, or how many of them there are. Protected or not, that's still not a comfortable place to be.

Things did get a little better over time. The head of HR, after seeing an interview I did on local TV following the second Vermont Burlesque Festival, actually tried to make it to one of my shows but it was sold out by the time she tried to get her tickets. I've also made a more recent friend at work who is aware, though again he found out in a round-about fashion. Over the course of some casual conversations I found out about his enjoyment of *The Rocky Horror Picture Show* and invited him to the annual Rocky Party that my then-wife and I hosted. I dress as Frank-N-Furter (Tim Curry's character) for those, so he basically saw me in drag at the party and it was a small jump to tell him it's a thing I do as a performer. So I had a couple of people at my work who were aware and for a time it made things a little better.

Unfortunately, they didn't stay that way. The head of HR left and the new one doesn't give me the vibe of somebody who would be as chill as the previous one. I know that seems like a vague reason for me to clam up, but I've learned to trust my gut on these things at this point. It doesn't help that with my longer and dyed hair, I keep it all stuffed up under a hat every day I'm in the office. In and of itself that's not awful, but it has started to weight on me as time as gone on.

In July of 2018, New Hampshire became the 20th state in the country to enshrine protections for gender identity into law. This, however, hasn't altered my presentation at my job. Because, as I noted earlier, it'd be very easy for them to find an allowable reason to cut me loose, and it would then be on me to try and prove that it was done because of gender identity discrimination.

Ultimately, unless you're working with people you would consider close friends, it's probably just easier for most of us to keep our dressing life out of our working life. The degree to which we have to be stringent about this will vary, but I realize looking back how lucky I was at that job in NYC where I had no fear about who knew. It's something I took for granted at the time and appreciate for its rarity now that I'm in a workplace that would become infinitely less comfortable if I was ever fully outed here.

THE CROSS DRESSING PARENT

So you cross dress, and as an adult that's your right to do as you see fit and to integrate it into your life in whatever way you want. But what if you have kids? Do you tell them? If so, at what age should you do it? How do you tell them? Does it cause more problems to hide it or be open? The answers to these questions are things that I'm still finding out as my daughter grows up, but I can offer what her mother and I have decided to do and our reasoning behind it.

I'm coming at this from the perspective of someone who was comfortable and more or less out of the closet before I ever had a child. I know that many dressers don't come into their own until later in life and may have the issue of older or even grown children to contend with. Regrettably, that situation lies too far outside my experience to be able to comment on. I'm not a child psychologist, but I am a parent and what I'm going to say is based off of what experience I have.

The first issue is whether or not your kids should know at all. This falls into a similar camp as what friends or family members you come out to, and I advise a similar yardstick. If this is primarily a bedroom and sexual activity for you then it's probably best that your children not be exposed to it. You wouldn't want your kids exposed openly to any other part of your sexual life, after all.

On the other hand, if this is just a part of your life and something you do (or want to do) without issues of shame or guilt, then I would strongly advise against hiding it. Hiding something automatically assigns a level of shame to it, both for you and your children. This shame causes guilt and can dampen your own ability to live as you choose, but more importantly you're effectively teaching your children that they have to hide who they really are. I'm sure some are thinking, "Well, if they don't know I'm hiding it, then how can they be learning that lesson?" It largely comes down the fundamental hypocrisy of it. Your life is simply going to be unbalanced if you preach "be yourself" while at the same time hide away fundamental truths of your own life. Not to mention the fact that if it is just a part of your normal life there's a good chance that eventually they will find out about it. When that happens it becomes similar to the spousal breach of trust situation. The discovery that you hid something like this for so long could undermine the life lessons you spent time trying to impart to your child. Now they might question what other secrets or lies you've been telling them. It's a bit like finding out that your parents who touted "just say 'no' to drugs" used to partake in illicit substances themselves when they were young, but neglected to mention that in all their anti-drug rhetoric. It just takes away their credibility in the face of simple hypocrisy.

These were some of the issues that Laura and I knew we were going to have to address. While we knew we didn't want to hide this side of me from our daughter, we also didn't want to turn her into some little crusader by overemphasizing the pride angle. That's only setting her up for confrontation when she inevitably encounters people who aren't ok with all of this. And that will happen sooner or later, but I'd prefer that she not be so young when it does. We determined it was best to just try and normalize my dressing as much as was possible. We did this in a few different ways.

My daughter wasn't quite two years old the first time she saw me in full dress. But I didn't just appear to her in makeup and wig and expect her to deal with it. Rather, we allowed her to watch the process, step by step, which was something she found quite interesting. This helped make it clear to her that Vera is not some other person. When I'm in dress I'm not "Auntie Vera" or some strange entity. I'm still "Daddy."

That was important for us, so as not to lay some overly confusing ideas on her. This isn't another person she had to think of differently, this is Daddy playing dress up.

The phrase "playing dress up" was another choice we made very deliberately. It's a term we settled on before our daughter was even born, largely because of its innocuous nature. The concern here wasn't so much about our daughter per se, but rather the other kids she would inevitably interact with. One thing that we've never wanted is for our daughter to be bullied because of something that has nothing to do with her. Of course, we don't want to see her bullied for any reason, but "my father is a cross dresser" gives other kids and even adults ammunition that I would never want used against my child. So framing it as "daddy plays dress up" puts it into a context that society as a whole can swallow. I play dress up, her mother plays dress up, and she plays dress up. And playing dress up doesn't always mean a skirt and heels. Sometimes I'll dress as the Doctor from *Doctor Who* while my daughter opts for Snow White. And other times she'll be a wolf and I'll be a princess. As she's gotten a bit older I've also framed it in terms of being a performer and getting into costume for a show. This is something that makes sense to her because both her mother and I are involved in local theater. She's always been around actors and people getting into costumes to perform.

So initially it was all just play, and it's framed and referred to in terms that will hopefully minimize any negative impact on my daughter's life. Because kids talk. That's just reality. She's going to mention all of this to some little friend at some point down the line, and I just want to be sure that it's presented in the best possible way. The alternative would have been to try to teach her that it's not ok to talk about with others. But just like trying to hide it from her at all, that assigns a sense of shame to it, and negates the idea of being true to one's self. Again, it is teaching "you can be anybody, but you can't be open about it." Not to mention that's quite a bit of responsibility and pressure to put on a child, the idea that they *must* keep some kind of family secret.

The whole thing has become a bit more transparent towards my daughter as she's entered into grade school. That has coincided with my allowing for a more gender-blended day-to-day look (when I'm not at work, at least) and at this point she doesn't even really notice much anymore. So at the very least, the idea of normalizing my gender expression seems to have worked. In her own way she gets to participate. Some days I let her pick out my earrings, which she enjoys. She also got to voice her opinion on the colors I added to my hair.

Is this the best way to handle all of this? It's difficult to say. It's the best we've come up with and it's worked out well so far. Maybe in 13 years I'll come back and write a whole other book just on this topic. But for now I feel that my family has found an approach that is working for us, and I wanted to share it so that those who need some form of guidance might have a starting point.

CHAPTER FOURTEEN

A QUIET REVELATION

I said very early on in this book that I feel like I never had a key moment in my life that I can point to and say, "*There!* That's where my gender-fluidity started!" However, I had a recent experience that has done a surprising amount to cement the headspace I'm now operating in. So it's story time again.

In 2017 I attended Boston Comic Con. This was the second time I'd gone to this particular convention. I'd been there the year before and had enjoyed it, but quickly found that I preferred the smaller setting of things like Vermont Comic Con. Boston was, frankly, a bit overwhelming, to say nothing of more expensive. But I went back, and I did so for one specific reason: to meet Tim Curry.

I'd never done the "pay extra money for a minute and a photograph with a celebrity" thing. And I thought I never would. There are plenty of actors I adore who attend these conventions and do those kinds of things. I have many a friend with pictures of themselves sharing space with key *Doctor Who* actors. And while that's my favorite show, I just didn't see it as being worth the money. But when I saw that Tim Curry would be in Boston, something clicked. I had to go. I would pay whatever extra I had to pay. This felt too important.

I've mentioned Tim Curry already in terms of his role in *Rocky Horror*, but that was far from his only impact on me growing up. I honestly think that he was the first actor who

I recognized as an actor rather than simply the character he was playing. I grew up on *Legend* and *Clue* at the same time as I was taking in *Star Wars*; regardless of the quality of any movie he was in, I was *always* happy to see Tim Curry. So this wasn't just about his gender-bending role.

I made it a day trip, drove down in the morning and didn't stick around all that long after I met him (as well as some other *Rocky Horror* alum that I didn't even realize would be there, so that was a nice bonus). I had thought about doing cosplay but decided against it. I didn't want to meet him as somebody else. I wanted to meet him as me. I did my makeup. I wore jeans and heeled boots. I wore a shirt, tie, and vest. I looked good but I didn't look like I was in costume.

I was running later than I wanted to be, so once I arrived I had to bolt straight to the line of folks who'd paid extra to meet Tim Curry. It was an eclectic group, some of whom were, in fact, in character cosplay from *Rocky Horror*. I stood in line for about an hour (which did not make my feet very happy thanks to the heeled boots). As I approached the front of the line I felt nervous. This was something I'd never done and might never do again. What if I said something stupid? What if I blew this?

Finally my time came. I approached him in his wheelchair (he'd had a stroke some years before and suffers from limited mobility). I told him that I'd loved his work for as long as I could remember. I'd thought I wouldn't bring up *Rocky Horror* because, given how I was dressed, it seemed too obvious and I didn't want him to think that was all I knew of his work. But I couldn't stop myself. I told him that I saw it at 13 and felt that I wouldn't be who I was today if I hadn't seen it.

He paused, and in a calmly genuine tone asked me, "And who are you?"

That was a question that from the wrong source and with the wrong inflection could have been devastating. It could have come across as more "who do you think you are?" or set off a panic in my head along the lines of "oh my god, I didn't properly introduce myself!" But that didn't happen. There was a regal feel to his words. It felt as if he was asking me the deepest possible version of that question. And I know that's probably me reading into it more than it deserves. But that doesn't matter, because that was how it felt.

And in response I told him, "I'm Nathaniel." Just like that. I didn't say I was Vera or Snow. I didn't even hesitate. I told him my birth name, something I had never done voluntarily when meeting somebody for the first time while presenting feminine or even mixed. I'd always given other names. Names I'd chosen. Names I could change. Never the one I've had since I came into this world. I stood next to one of my idols, in makeup and false lashes, and told him the name that's on my driver's license. And that moment became a turning point for much of what has come since.

For the first time, I didn't feel the rigid separation of a name. What Vera is has been changing over time. She's changed styles, changed attitudes, and gone for less outright feminine looks as time has gone on. But up to that point, despite all the changes, she was still very much separate in my mind. And in that one instant, Vera and Nathaniel snapped together. Vera had always been an aspect of me, but had not always felt like a complete person. This one question and this one answer made me feel a sense of joy and pride in myself that was new. It wasn't pride in Vera as a persona or a performer or a model. It was pride in me, just me, whatever that may be.

I'm not exaggerating when I say that was a life-changing experience. Plus, he told me that he liked my earrings.

Meeting Tim Curry at the 2017 Boston Comic Con.

IT'S OK TO EVOLVE

If there's one thing I've learned throughout my life that keeps me sane, it's this: change is natural. It's aggravating how long it took me to work on this book but things about my life and how dressing fits into it kept changing and I had to keep going back and updating or adding new sections (the one you just read being the most recent). But as annoying as that is for trying to create a record, it is the truth of my existence.

I've gone from a young boy with no clear point or goal to my dressing, to a confused young adult whose emotions collided with sexual desires and gender identity making everything even harder to sort out, to an adult with a pretty clear dividing wall between my masculine and feminine sides, to somebody looking down the barrel of middle age who has willingly let that same dividing wall fall into total disrepair. I expect in another few years things will be in yet another state altogether.

I don't know where I'm going to end up. I don't know the destination of any of this, or if there even is one. Some things that I did between the first and final drafts of this book that I didn't think I would ever do included piercing my ears, buying feminine frames for my glasses, getting my hair styled in a more overtly feminine fashion, getting my hair dyed with turquoise and purple highlights, working with my doctor on hormone adjustments, and, very recently, effectively "coming out" as Vera on my primary social media account. Some of these I've talked about already, but those last two I'll discuss here.

I waited *way* too long to get a primary care physician. It was just one of those things that was a pain in the butt to figure out and I stalled literally for years on it. When I finally got one I was very open about my gender-fluidity. Part of this was because I was idly experimenting with "supplements" that claimed vaguely feminizing properties. Which, to be clear, is not something I recommend. The supplement market is largely unregulated and most of these things have little to no effect (I never saw any impact). It was more curiosity driving my experimentation with them than an actual objective for myself. But I wanted to be sure my doctor was fully aware of what it was I was taking. It was his suggestion that we try a proper prescription hormone adjustment. Now, those who are planning a full transition from male to female go on a combination of estrogen and testosterone blockers. I am currently on testosterone blockers but not on estrogen. The theory here is that we're trying to get my default setting to be something close to a proper neutral. Because no matter how I may feel on any given day, I'm still physically male first and foremost. When I'm in a masculine mood, that's all well and good, but if I'm in a feminine mindset it takes a fair amount of work to feel like I've gotten myself into a representation of how I'm feeling. So if my starting point is closer to the middle rather than decidedly male, it makes going in either direction an equal task rather than one being more work than the other.

At the time of this writing I'm only just starting to see notable physical impacts from this. My body hair comes in slower and lighter than it used to. I rarely have spontaneous erections (though overall sexual function is unaffected). My nipples are much more sensitive and have increased in size slightly. Normally there'd be concern about possible sterility, but I was already planning to get a vasectomy anyway. As far as I'm concerned I already have the perfect kid and I don't expect I'd hit the jackpot twice.

All of this was a pretty serious step because since my 20s I've been of the mindset that I don't want a full, permanent transition to life as a woman. And for the record, that hasn't changed. I didn't begin this as a first step toward that end goal, because as I said, I don't know where this is going. It's part of my continued exploration of me and what it means to be me. I may decide to stop taking testosterone blockers. I may stay on them and nothing else. I may decide to stop taking them and try only estrogen on its own. I don't know, and right now I'm ok with that.

In regards to the "coming out" online, that was the culmination of a number of things. By early 2018, my family and pretty much all my friends were aware of my gender-fluidity, even if it wasn't something they'd witnessed firsthand. But I also had a fairly public side where that wasn't known. I mentioned my Vera Wylde YouTube channel, but there's another that I've had for almost as long called Council of Geeks. It's mostly me in a masculine presentation ranting about geeky things like *Doctor Who*, *Star Wars*, superheroes, etc. It was a pretty small channel for quite a while. But over the course of 2017 it jumped from 1,200 subscribers to 10,000. Not only was this a subscriber number I never expected to hit, but it put Council of Geeks past Vera Wylde in terms of online visibility. This worried me.

There had actually been a few people who knew me as Vera and stumbled upon Council of Geeks. And for folks who knew Vera first, it's not really all that shocking. Since I talk about how I don't live full-time as a woman, finding something where I present masculine fits what's already known about me for people who follow Vera. But when Council of Geeks became the bigger channel I worried about what would happen when inevitably somebody who knew that channel first found Vera. And that was much more likely to cause confusion, or even anger. The last thing I wanted was somebody "revealing" the connection between the two channels like it was some kind of secret. Because no matter what, if my talking about it was in response to somebody else bringing it up first it would look like I had been hiding it. It would look like I was ashamed. And I'm not, and never will be. So I had to be the one to say it first. This had to happen on my terms, and the longer I waited and the bigger the channel got, the more likely it was that somebody would beat me to it.

So to celebrate 10,000 subscribers I put together a Q&A video, addressing common questions I got about Council of Geeks as well as soliciting new questions. The last one that I answered (and one I had been getting sporadically for almost a year by that point) was "are you Vera Wylde?" I switched to my cat eye frames and took off the flat cap that had become my signature look on the channel so I could show off my styled and dyed hair. I talked for about 10 minutes about my gender-fluidity on a channel that had never broached that topic. I uploaded the video before going to bed and did not know what I was going to wake up to.

To this day I'm still bowled over by the response. So much support. So many kind words. And nothing harsher in the comments section than "I don't get it, but it's fine." I'm writing this some months after the video went up and there are a grand total of three down votes on it. I get a harsher reaction than that to, well, almost everything else I ever put up. Sometimes, and it is a rarity, the Internet surprises you in a positive way.

This was followed up a few months later with a post to my masculine Facebook account (because there's always been one for Nathaniel and one for Vera) on March 31st, which is Trans Day of Visibility. I put up a selfie of myself in makeup with feminine glasses and a brief explanation that my sense of gender doesn't stay put and some people know me as Vera rather than Nathaniel, ending it with: "This is me, being visible." Even though pretty much all my close friends were aware of this, I have a ton of casual acquaintances on Facebook, as do most of us I expect. That post received a similarly positive response to the Q&A video and it removed any lingering doubt or awkwardness of trying to remember who did or didn't know.

One of the freeing things about being at peace with not knowing the destination of my gender journey is that I can look back at the places I've been and feel like I was largely in the right place at the right time. For those who know they want to transition or otherwise have a very firm idea of what they want their gender to be, they tend to look back on times when that wasn't the case with regret. Trans folk who were closeted or unsupported or lacked the resources to transition so often look back on the times prior to transition as lost time. It's another life altogether that many prefer to not dwell on. "If only I'd been the real me sooner." I feel like I've always been the real me. It's just that the real me is constantly changing. When dressing was something that I did in private, that's what I needed it to be. When I had that solid wall built up between my feminine and masculine sides and wasn't exploring the middle ground, it was where I needed to be at the time. I've evolved past that, but I don't look back at it with regret or a sense of having done it wrong up until now.

I suppose that's the thing about being a dresser with no intention to live full-time as a woman or undergo a full physical gender transition: this is a journey and not a destination. I don't do this in the hope that one day I'll get to be a woman every minute of every day. It's not *for* anything. It's not a sexual kink, even though it can make me feel sexy. It just is. This is me. This is a thing that I do, and it's important to who I am no matter what form it is currently taking. I suppose the one constant is that this part of myself has never gone away completely. And I wouldn't want it to.

I'm proud of Vera, as a performer, as a writer, and just as a person. But I now also feel that she and I aren't just occupying the same space. We are, in fact, coming together. Sometimes I'll still go all masculine or all feminine, and either one is fine. Either one is me. I have no shame attached to the fact that half of my closet is taken up with dresses and wigs. But I also don't get depressed that the other half is taken up with button down shirts and suits. These are just some of the parts that make up who I am. And I like me, no matter which aspect of me might be looking back from the mirror.

SPECIAL THANKS

As I sit down to prepare for some acknowledgments, I'm almost overwhelmed by it. The number of people I have to thank for helping me to arrive at this point in my life is probably incalculable. The people who made this actual book possible is probably a more manageable list.

I want to thank my YouTube subscribers who've come to me with their questions and their encouragement for years. They were the first ones to show me that it isn't just a handful of people out there who are seeking this kind of information.

I want to thank Cracked for offering me my first wide-reaching audience by publishing my joke-tinged article in the spring of 2015.

I want to thank my mother, for being one of my most stalwart supporters in all things. And for raising me in a home where, no matter what was going on with me, I never had any fear that she would reject or stop loving me.

I want to thank Laura, my former wife and mother of my child. Not only for all the support she's given (and continues to give) me, but for giving her blessing to my sharing parts of our personal story with all of you.

I want to thank my friend Giuliana for being the first person, upon being told about this book concept, to do more than nod and go, "That's not a bad idea." Her unbridled "when can I buy it?!?" enthusiasm was not only encouraging, but a useful guilt trip because it made me want to see this through just so she could do that.

I want to thank the Green Mountain Cabaret and the burlesque community of Vermont for helping ensure that I always had a home on stage. And for putting up with my tendency to hog the makeup mirrors.

I want to thank Syd London for being a wonderful friend, and a huge supporter of every creative endeavor I've ever undertaken. Not to mention contributing some of the amazing photography featured in this book.

I want to thank my partner Lis for her kindness, her openness, and her taste in wine (because writing is hard and I need to unwind somehow).

I want to thank all my other friends and family for accepting me as they've learned about this aspect of my life. For being respectful with their questions and open with their arms.

I want to thank my editor Sarah Brown for her eagerness about the project and for making my first time working with a professional editor so smooth.

And finally, I want to thank the people who donated to my Kickstarter campaign, which is what allowed me to actually be able to hire Sarah in the first place.

This book as you've read it wouldn't have been possible without the backing of:
Kaylee A.
Michel Siskoid Albert
Mary Aschenberg
Cara Beaudoin
Adora Bourbon
Gregg Carpenter

Clarke Collins
Meg Cossaboom
Tracy Dale
erica dreisbach
Ellane C.C. Villainous Vixens
Mark Fern
Teresa Fresina
Adrian Garneau
Joshua James Gervais
GFunk!
Isabelle "Shotgun" Godin
Kale Irish
Jeri
Alistair J. Kraft
Libby Lawless
Tyra Mandahl
Erika Martin
Kevin Montanaro
Nan Murat
Amanda Nobil
Mark Pinto
Brandon "Beatrix" Purvis
Sarah Springer
Tanit Richards
Jon, Kirty and Morgan Van Luling
Doctor Vu

70645057R00146